Revised

Patchwork Minus Mathwork

Whether you enjoy math or absolutely cringe at the thought of working with figures, you'll love this book. We've done all the tedious mathematical work so that you can more quickly decide how much fabric and batting to purchase for your patchwork quilts.

Before you try to use our charts for your own personal quilt, read through the information given in How to Use This Book and we'll help you plan an example in the Planning a Quilt section. By reading through the steps and planning an example full-size quilt, you will become familiar with how the charts work. This will save you the time of experimenting on your own.

If you prefer to work in meters and centimeters, we've included an easy-to-use conversion chart that includes metric equivalents on page 44.

Table of Contents

How to Use This Book **2**

Planning a Quilt **3**

- Standard Mattress Sizes **9**
- Suggested Quilt Sizes **9**

Quilt Sizes & Number of Blocks **10**

- Straight Set **10**
- Straight Set With Sashing **11**
- Straight Set With Alternating Squares **15**
- Diagonal Set **16**
- Diagonal Set With Sashing **17**
- Diagonal Set With Alternating Squares **22**

Figuring Yardage **24**

- Rectangles **24**
- Squares **27**
- Half-Square Triangles **30**
- Quarter-Square Triangles **32**
- Sashing Strips **35**
- Diamonds (60 degree) **38**
- Diamonds (45 degree) **39**
- Borders **40**
- Quilt Backing **40**
- Diagonal Measurement of Blocks **41**
- Batting **41**
- Binding **42**

Metric Conversions, ***44*** • *Quilt Worksheet,* ***45*** • *Shopping List,* ***48***

How to Use This Book

Patchwork Minus Mathwork is a collection of charts that will help you to plan a quilt and figure yardages without doing the math.

Go through the steps in Planning a Quilt, pages 3–9, along with the Figuring Yardage charts, pages 24–43, then use the Quilt Worksheet, pages 45–47, to figure yardages you will need for your quilt. When you are finished, write the amounts on the Shopping List on page 48, and you are ready to go to your local quilt shop or fabric store, or visit your favorite online fabric source.

Although it would be impossible to include every size in the Quilt Sizes & Number of Blocks charts on pages 10–23, there are enough choices that you will surely find one that suits your needs. These are meant to be guidelines for planning a quilt, not hard-and-fast rules.

Once you have chosen a block, look through the charts and find a size that is compatible with your needs. The chart will tell you how many blocks you will need, what size they should be, and anything else (sashing strips, sashing squares, plain squares, or setting triangles) you will need to complete your quilt. Keep in mind that the quilt sizes in the charts do not include borders. If you want to add borders to make fewer or larger blocks, you can still use the information in the charts.

A quilt with a specific block layout will have the same information no matter what size the block is. For example, a diagonal-set quilt with a block layout of four by five will always have 32 blocks and 14 setting triangles as noted in the chart on page 16. Just be aware that your quilt measurement may not be the same as our example.

Hint

Remember this good rule of thumb: It is always best to add at least ¼ yard to all measurements for insurance. It is better to have leftover fabric than it is to run out of a particular fabric and not be able to purchase more.

In addition, the edge of the fabric usually needs to be straightened before cutting strips. If many strips are cut from the same fabric, it may need to be straightened several times to square up edges again. This will add a little to the amount of fabric needed.

Precut Fabric Sizes

The following sizes were used to calculate numbers in the precut charts in this book.

- *Jelly Roll—2½" x 42"*
- *Bali Pop—2½" x 42"*
- *Honey Buns—1½" x 42"*
- *Fat Rolls—5" x 42"*
- *Nickels/Charms—5" squares*
- *Layer Cakes/Dimes—10" squares*
- *Sweet Sixteens—16" squares*
- *Fat Quarters—18" x 21"*

The yardage charts in this book are based on a fabric width of 40" except for the precut charts. This allows for variances in fabric width off the bolt and shrinkage from washing. Simple layouts shown with the charts show the most efficient use of fabric.

Precut fabrics such as Jelly Rolls™ (2½" x 42"), Layer Cakes/Dimes (10" x 10" squares) and fat quarters (18" x 21"), are popular today, so we have included them in this book for your convenience.

It is easiest to use a rotary cutter, mat and appropriate ruler to first cut strips the correct width. Then subcut the strips into squares, rectangles, triangles or diamonds as needed.

If using templates, use the same layout and butt the edges of the template to those of the previous piece to use as little fabric as possible.

The Border and Binding yardage charts include several sizes of borders, but if the size you want is not included, you can still use the charts. Just go to the next widest border and buy the suggested yardage knowing that you will have a little left over. Also, if the perimeter of your quilt is not one of those listed in the chart, always go to the next highest number and use that yardage.

Planning a Quilt

What Size?

When you are preparing to make a quilt, one of the first things you need to establish is what size it is going to be. Either measure your mattress or use the Standard Mattress Sizes chart on page 9 as a guide. Many of today's mattresses are thicker than those in the past. For this type of mattress you will need a longer drop. The size of the mattress top measurement is standard and has not changed.

For the example, we are going to make a quilt to fit a full-size bed with a 12" drop. Look at the Suggested Quilt Sizes chart on page 9 to find that a full-size quilt with a 12" drop should measure around 78" x 97".

Choose Your Block & Layout

The next step is to find your favorite block, decide how big it needs to be, and how many you will have to make. Keep in mind that you must make at least enough blocks to cover the top of the mattress with a little overhang. The remaining length and width will be added with borders.

We will use the block shown in Figure 1. It is a Nine-Patch with triangles and two different sizes of squares.

Figure 1

What size should the block be? We know that the quilt we want will measure about 78" x 97". Look at the charts for Quilt Sizes & Number of Blocks on pages 10–23. For a straight-set, full-size quilt with measurements close to the example, the chart shows that you will need to make 63 blocks that finish 11" square. The quilt will be 77" x 99" with seven blocks across and nine blocks down as shown in Layout 1a. But perhaps you don't want to make that many blocks, and besides, 11" doesn't divide evenly for a Nine-Patch. There are several options.

Layout 1a

Option 1: Make larger blocks: If you make 12" blocks, you only need 56 blocks (seven across and eight down) to make a quilt measuring 84" x 96" (Layout 1b). That still seems like a lot of sewing.

Layout 1b

Option 2: Add borders: The 12" block size is good because it can be divided evenly for our Nine-Patch. Eliminate one vertical row and add borders to give the desired size. Now you only need to make 48 blocks (six across and eight down). The quilt without borders will now measure 72" x 96" as shown in Layout 1c. If you add a 3"-wide border, your quilt will measure 78" x 102".

Layout 1c

Option 3: Eliminate another vertical row as well as a horizontal row so that you only need 35 blocks (five across and seven down) and add another border. Your quilt center without borders will measure 60" x 84" (Layout 1d). Add borders to achieve the sizes needed.

Layout 1d

Option 4: If that still seems like a lot, you can add sashing. If you make 3"-finished sashing strips, you can eliminate another horizontal and vertical row and only make 24 blocks (four across and six down). The quilt center will now finish at 63" x 93" (Layout 2). Add borders to achieve the size needed.

Layout 2

Option 5: What if you substitute plain squares for some of the blocks? This will reduce the number of blocks you need to stitch. It is best to have an odd number of blocks in each direction so that a pieced block will be in every corner for a more balanced look. So, substitute every other block with a plain square, and you only need to make 18 blocks.

Layout 3

That's a lot less than 63 in the original plan. The quilt center will now measure 60" x 84" (Layout 3). Borders may be added to achieve the size needed.

Option 6: So far all of the samples show blocks set straight across, and up and down in rows. What if you like the blocks set on the diagonal or on point? The 12" block we are using has a diagonal measurement of 17" (see Diagonal Measurement of Blocks chart on page 41). Using this layout, you will need 32 blocks. You will also need side or setting and corner triangles. Refer to the Quilt Sizes & Number of Blocks chart for Diagonal Set quilts on page 16 for the number of setting triangles needed. The quilt center will measure 68" x 85" (Layout 4). Add borders to achieve the size needed.

Layout 4

Option 7: If you add 2½"-finished sashing strips in between the diagonal blocks, you only need to make 18 blocks. The quilt center will measure 65¼" x 85¾" (Layout 5). Add borders to achieve the size needed.

Option 8: Replace alternate blocks with plain squares, and you will need to make 20 blocks and 12 plain squares. The quilt center will measure 68" x 85" (Layout 6). Add borders to achieve the size needed.

Layout 5

Layout 6

How Much Fabric to Buy

Blocks

Once you have chosen the layout, figure out how many of each shape you will need, then you can find the yardage needed for the quilt. Use graph paper and colored pencils to color your layout to decide the placement of fabrics or colors. There can be several different ways to color the layout as shown in the following blocks and layouts. Notice how changing the color placement within the block can change the entire look of the quilt.

There are eight dark and eight medium-light 2" squares, one dark 4" square, four light 4" triangles and four dark 4" triangles in each block. Therefore, for a straight-set quilt with 12" blocks, you will need the following using the color arrangement of Block 1:

- 8 x 35 = 280 each dark and medium-light 2" squares (cut size 2½")
- 1 x 35 = 35 dark 4" squares (cut size 4½")
- 4 x 35 = 140 each light and dark 4" triangles (cut 4⅞" squares in half on one diagonal)

Now that you know the cut size and the number of shapes needed for your quilt, you can figure the yardage amounts for each fabric. Use the Figuring Yardage charts starting on page 24.

For the example quilt (Block 1 Quilt Layout, below), there are 280 dark 2" squares. Look down the first column of the Squares chart on page 27 until you find 2". Look across and see that the cut size of the squares will be 2½". Now look across that row until you see the number of squares that are needed for your quilt. If the exact number is not shown, go to the next highest number. In this example it will be 288. Look straight up to the top line and see that it will take 1¼ yards to result in 280 squares cut 2½".

You will also need 1¼ yards for 280 medium-light squares.

For the 35 dark 4" squares, use the same chart to find that you will need ¾ yard of the dark fabric.

For the 140 dark triangles, use the Half-Square Triangle chart, page 30. Look down the first column until you see 4"; you will need to cut squares 4⅞". (You will get two triangles for every square cut and the outside edges will be on the straight of the

Block 1

Block 1 Quilt Layout

Block 2

Block 2 Quilt Layout

Block 3 Quilt Layout

Block 3

Block 4

Block 4 Quilt Layout

Block 5

Block 5 Quilt Layout

Block 6

Block 6 Quilt Layout

Block 7

Block 7 Quilt Layout

grain.) Look straight across the row until you see 140 or the next highest number, which is 144. Now look at the top of the column and see that it will take 1¼ yards dark fabric for your triangles. You will need the same amount for the light triangles.

Borders

Simple Borders

Your next decision is to decide on the size of the borders. The quilt has 35 blocks set five across and seven down. The blocks finish at 12"; therefore, the quilt top should measure 60" x 84". Once sewn together, your quilt-top measurement may differ slightly from the mathematical measurement if your ¼" seam allowance was slightly off. Don't worry about the size difference as long as all of your blocks are the same size.

Since we would like our quilt to measure around 78" x 97", and our layout works out to only 60" x 84" (finished), we will have to add borders. We need an additional 18" for the width and 13" for the length. It is better to use the larger of the two measurements, which is 18". Dividing 18" by 2 (since there are border strips on each side) means that your border should be 9" wide when finished. There are several ways to achieve this: two borders that finish at 3" and 6" wide; three borders that finish at 2", 3" and 4" wide; or two borders that finish at 4" and 5" wide. There are other combinations as well.

Go to the Borders yardage chart on page 40 to figure out how much yardage you will need. If you choose the 3"-, 2"- and 4"-wide borders, the yardage requirements will be as follows:

Quilt measures 60½" x 84½" (seam allowance included).

For the 3" border:

Measurement for the side borders:

- 84½" + 84½" = 169" total

Measurement for the top and bottom borders:

- 60½" + 60½" + 3" + 3" + 3" + 3" (border totals) = 133" total

Add the total inches for sides, and top and bottom borders for total number of inches needed:

- 169" + 133" = 302" of border strips

According to the Borders yardage chart on page 40, you will need ⅞ yard of fabric for 302" of border strips.

> ***Note:** To figure the yardage mathematically, divide the total inches of border strips by 40" (the usable fabric width). Multiply that number by the cut width of the border strips.*
>
> • 302" ÷ 40 = 7.55 strips rounded up to 8 strips needed.
>
> • 3½" x 8 strips = 28" or ⅞ yard.

For the 2" border:
Recalculate the quilt size to include the first border. It should measure 66½" x 90½" including seam allowances.

Measurement for the side borders:

• 90½" + 90½" = 181" total

Measurement for the top and bottom borders:

• 66½" + 66½" + 2" + 2" + 2" + 2" = 141" total

Add the total inches for sides, and top and bottom borders for total number of inches needed:

• 181" + 141" = 322" of border strips

According to the Borders yardage chart on page 40, you will need ⅝ yard of this border fabric.

For the 4" border:
Recalculate the quilt size to include the first and second borders. It should measure 70½" x 94½" including seam allowances.

Measurement for the side borders:

• 94½" + 94½" = 189" total

Measurement for the top and bottom borders:

• 70½" + 70½" + 4" + 4" + 4" + 4" (center measurement plus the width of the side borders on both ends of the top and bottom) = 157" total

Add total inches for sides, and top and bottom borders for total number of inches needed:

• 189" + 157" = 346" of border strips

According to the Borders yardage chart on page 40, you will need 1⅛ yards of this border fabric.

When all the borders are attached, your quilt top with borders will measure approximately 78½" x 102½".

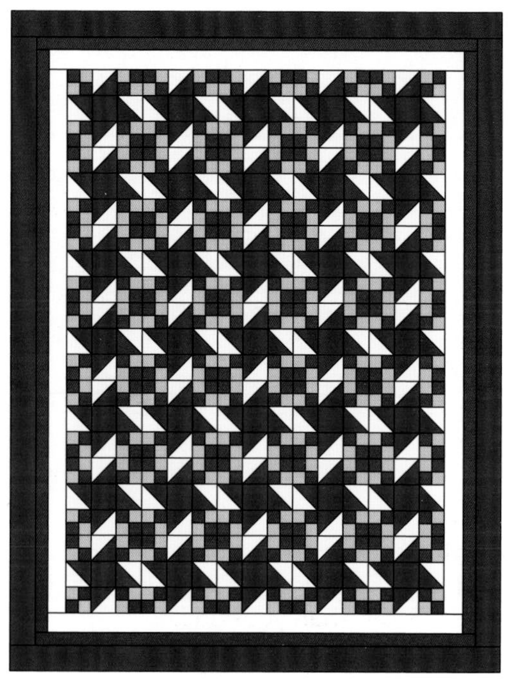

Quilt Top

Mitered Borders

To figure yards for mitered borders, measure the length and width of the quilt—the sample quilt is 60½" x 84½". ***Note:** An extra 4" is added to the length of each border strip for ease in mitering corners.*

For the 3" border:
Measurement for side borders:

• 84½" + 3" + 3" + 4" = 94½" total; multiply total by 2: 94½" x 2 = 189" for two side borders

Measurement for top and bottom borders:

• 60½" + 3" + 3" + 4" = 70½" total; multiply total by 2: 70½" x 2 = 141" for top and bottom borders

Add total inches for sides, and top and bottom borders for total number of inches needed:

• 189" + 141" = 330" total for border strips

According to the yardage chart for Borders on page 40, you will need ⅞ yard of fabric for the 3"-wide border.

Repeat the process for remaining borders, recalculating quilt size after each border addition.

Backing & Batting

The borders are on—your quilt top is finished. Now you have to do the quilting. Before you can quilt, the quilt has to be layered.

First, figure out how much backing fabric you will need. Turn to the yardage chart for Quilt Backing on page 40 and look for the quilt measurement closest to your quilt's size (78½" x 102½"), which is 88" x 104". ***Note:*** *Always use a measurement in which both numbers are equal to or larger than your own quilt measurements.*

You will need 7¾ yards of backing fabric according to the chart. This yardage will have to be cut into three equal-length sections and sewn together as in layout e on page 40.

You will also need batting. Packaged batting comes in many types and sizes. Choose one that is 3"–4" larger on all sides than your quilt.

The most common packaged batting sizes are:

Crib	45" x 60"
Twin	72" x 90"
Full	81" x 96"
Queen	90" x 108"
King	120" x 120"

Batting also comes off the bolt: batting widths range from 22"–120".

Note: *If you have to use two or more lengths of batting to get the desired length or width, butt the ends against each other and whipstitch together. Be sure there is no lump where the pieces meet.*

Standard Mattress Sizes

Mattress	Standard Size
Crib	23" x 46"
Twin	39" x 75"
Full	54" x 75"
Queen	60" x 80"
King	76" x 80"

Binding

Once the quilt is quilted, the final step is to add binding. There are many different widths as well as single-fold and double-fold bindings. Choose a double-fold 2¼" cut-width binding for the example quilt. Look at the chart for Double-Fold Binding on page 42 to find the 2¼" cut width. Measure the perimeter of your quilt. For the example quilt measuring 78½" x 102½", the perimeter would be 362". That is the number of inches of 2¼"-wide binding strips that you will need for the quilt. Add 12" to the total for joining the strips—374" total.

According to the chart for Double-Fold Binding on page 42, you will need ⅝ yard cut into (10) 2¼"-wide crosswise strips.

Note: *To figure the yards mathematically, divide the total number of inches of binding strips by 40" (the usable fabric width). Multiply that number by the cut width of the fabric: 374" divided by 40" = 9.35 rounded up to 10 strips needed. To figure yardage needed, mulitply 10 x 2¼" to equal 22.5" or ⅝ yard.*

Now that you have gone through the steps of planning a quilt, you can use the Quilt Worksheet on pages 45–47 to plan your own quilt.

Suggested Quilt Sizes

Amount of Drop	Twin	Full	Queen	King
12" drop	63" x 97"	78" x 97"	84" x 102"	100" x 102"
14" drop	67" x 99"	82" x 99"	88" x 104"	104" x 104"
16" drop	71" x 101"	86" x 101"	92" x 106"	108" x 106"
18" drop	75" x 103"	90" x 103"	96" x 108"	112" x 108"
20" drop	79" x 105"	94" x 105"	100" x 110"	116" x 110"
22" drop	83" x 107"	98" x 107"	104" x 112"	120" x 112"
24" drop	87" x 109"	102" x 109"	108" x 114"	124" x 114"
26" drop	91" x 111"	106" x 111"	112" x 116"	128" x 116"
28" drop	95" x 113"	110" x 113"	116" x 118"	132" x 118"
30" drop	99" x 115"	114" x 115"	120" x 120"	136" x 120"

Quilt Sizes & Number of Blocks

***Note:** All sizes are finished sizes unless noted otherwise.*

Straight Set

Crib Sizes (Without Borders)

Block Size	Block Layout	No. of Blocks	Quilt Size
4"	6 x 11	66	24" x 44"
5"	5 x 9	45	25" x 45"
6"	4 x 8	32	24" x 48"
7"	4 x 7	28	28" x 49"
8"	3 x 6	18	24" x 48"

Twin Sizes (Without Borders)

Block Size	Block Layout	No. of Blocks	Quilt Size
5"	13 x 20	260	65" x 100"
6"	11 x 17	187	66" x 102"
7"	9 x 14	126	63" x 98"
7"	10 x 14	140	70" x 98"
8"	8 x 12	96	64" x 96"
9"	7 x 11	77	63" x 99"
10"	6 x 10	60	60" x 100"
11"	6 x 9	54	66" x 99"
12"	5 x 7	35	60" x 84"
12"	5 x 8	40	60" x 96"
13"	5 x 7	35	65" x 91"
14"	4 x 7	28	56" x 98"

Full Sizes (Without Borders)

Block Size	Block Layout	No. of Blocks	Quilt Size
5"	16 x 20	320	80" x 100"
6"	14 x 16	224	84" x 96"
7"	12 x 14	168	84" x 98"
8"	10 x 12	120	80" x 96"
9"	9 x 11	99	81" x 99"
10"	8 x 10	80	80" x 100"
11"	7 x 9	63	77" x 99"
12"	6 x 7	42	72" x 84"
12"	7 x 8	56	84" x 96"
13"	6 x 8	48	78" x 104"
14"	6 x 7	42	84" x 98"
14"	4 x 7	28	56" x 98"

Queen Sizes (Without Borders)

Block Size	Block Layout	No. of Blocks	Quilt Size
5"	18 x 21	378	90" x 105"
6"	15 x 17	255	90" x 102"
7"	13 x 15	195	91" x 105"
8"	11 x 13	143	88" x 104"
9"	10 x 12	120	90" x 108"
10"	9 x 10	90	90" x 100"
11"	8 x 9	72	88" x 99"
12"	7 x 9	63	84" x 108"
13"	7 x 8	56	91" x 104"
14"	6 x 7	42	84" x 98"
15"	6 x 7	42	90" x 105"
16"	6 x 6	36	96" x 96"
17"	5 x 6	30	85" x 102"
18"	5 x 6	30	90" x 108"

King Sizes (Without Borders)

Block Size	Block Layout	No. of Blocks	Quilt Size
5"	21 x 21	441	105" x 105"
6"	17 x 17	289	102" x 102"
7"	15 x 15	225	105" x 105"
8"	13 x 13	169	104" x 104"
9"	12 x 12	144	108" x 108"
10"	10 x 10	100	100" x 100"
11"	9 x 9	81	99" x 99"
12"	9 x 9	81	108" x 108"
13"	8 x 8	64	104" x 104"
14"	8 x 8	64	112" x 112"
14"	7 x 7	49	98" x 98"
15"	7 x 7	49	105" x 105"
16"	6 x 6	36	96" x 96"
17"	6 x 6	36	102" x 102"
18"	6 x 6	36	108" x 108"
18"	5 x 5	25	90" x 90"
19"	5 x 5	25	95" x 95"
20"	5 x 5	25	100" x 100"
21"	5 x 5	25	105" x 105"
21"	4 x 4	16	84" x 84"

Straight Set With Sashing

Twin Sizes (Without Borders)

1" Sashing

Block Size	Block Layout	No. of Blocks	No. of Sashing Strips	No. of Sashing Squares	Quilt Size
5"	11 x 17	187	402	216	67" x 103"
6"	9 x 14	126	275	150	64" x 99"
7"	8 x 12	96	212	117	65" x 97"

1½" Sashing

Block Size	Block Layout	No. of Blocks	No. of Sashing Strips	No. of Sashing Squares	Quilt Size
5"	10 x 15	150	325	176	66½" x 99"
6"	8 x 13	104	229	126	61½" x 99"
7"	7 x 12	84	187	104	61" x 103½"
8"	6 x 10	60	136	77	58½" x 96½"

2" Sashing

Block Size	Block Layout	No. of Blocks	No. of Sashing Strips	No. of Sashing Squares	Quilt Size
5"	8 x 14	112	246	135	58" x 100"
6"	8 x 12	96	212	117	66" x 98"
7"	7 x 11	77	172	96	65" x 101"
8"	6 x 10	60	136	77	62" x 102"
9"	6 x 9	54	123	70	68" x 101"
10"	5 x 8	40	93	54	62" x 98"

Twin Sizes (Without Borders)

2½" Sashing

Block Size	Block Layout	No. of Blocks	No. of Sashing Strips	No. of Sashing Squares	Quilt Size
6"	7 x 12	84	187	104	62" x 104½"
7"	6 x 10	60	136	77	59½" x 97½"
8"	6 x 9	54	123	70	65½" x 97"
9"	5 x 8	40	93	54	60" x 94½"
10"	5 x 8	40	93	54	65" x 102½"

3" Sashing

Block Size	Block Layout	No. of Blocks	No. of Sashing Strips	No. of Sashing Squares	Quilt Size
6"	7 x 11	77	172	96	66" x 102"
7"	6 x 10	60	136	77	63" x 103"
8"	5 x 9	45	104	60	58" x 102"
9"	5 x 8	40	93	54	63" x 99"
10"	5 x 7	35	82	48	68" x 94"
11"	5 x 7	35	82	48	73" x 103"
12"	4 x 6	24	58	35	63" x 93"

Full Sizes (Without Borders)

1" Sashing

Block Size	Block Layout	No. of Blocks	No. of Sashing Strips	No. of Sashing Squares	Quilt Size
6"	12 x 14	168	362	195	85" x 99"
7"	10 x 12	120	262	143	81" x 97"
8"	9 x 11	99	218	120	82" x 100"
9"	8 x 10	80	178	99	81" x 101"

1½" Sashing

Block Size	Block Layout	No. of Blocks	No. of Sashing Strips	No. of Sashing Squares	Quilt Size
5"	13 x 16	208	445	238	86" x 105½"
6"	11 x 13	143	310	168	84" x 99"
7"	9 x 12	108	237	130	78" x 103½"
8"	9 x 11	99	218	120	87" x 106"
9"	8 x 10	80	178	99	85½" x 106½"
10"	7 x 9	63	142	80	82" x 105"
11"	7 x 8	56	127	72	89" x 101½"

Full Sizes (Without Borders)

2" Sashing

Block Size	Block Layout	No. of Blocks	No. of Sashing Strips	No. of Sashing Squares	Quilt Size
5"	12 x 14	168	362	195	86" x 100"
6"	10 x 12	120	262	143	82" x 98"
7"	9 x 11	99	218	120	83" x 101"
8"	8 x 10	80	178	99	82" x 102"
9"	7 x 9	63	142	80	79" x 101"
10"	7 x 8	56	127	72	86" x 98"
11"	6 x 8	48	110	63	80" x 106"
12"	6 x 7	42	97	56	86" x 100"

2½" Sashing

Block Size	Block Layout	No. of Blocks	No. of Sashing Strips	No. of Sashing Squares	Quilt Size
6"	10 x 12	120	262	143	87½" x 104½"
7"	9 x 11	99	218	120	88" x 107"
8"	8 x 10	80	178	99	86½" x 107½"
9"	7 x 9	63	142	80	83" x 106"
10"	6 x 8	48	110	63	77½" x 102½"
11"	6 x 7	42	97	56	83½" x 97"
12"	6 x 7	42	97	56	89½" x 104"

3" Sashing

Block Size	Block Layout	No. of Blocks	No. of Sashing Strips	No. of Sashing Squares	Quilt Size
6"	9 x 11	99	218	120	84" x 102"
7"	8 x 10	80	178	99	83" x 103"
8"	7 x 9	63	142	80	80" x 102"
9"	7 x 8	56	127	72	87" x 99"
10"	6 x 8	48	110	63	81" x 107"
11"	6 x 7	42	97	56	87" x 101"
12"	5 x 7	35	82	48	78" x 108"
13"	5 x 6	30	71	42	83" x 99"
14"	4 x 5	20	49	30	71" x 88"

Queen Sizes (Without Borders)

1" Sashing

Block Size	Block Layout	No. of Blocks	No. of Sashing Strips	No. of Sashing Squares	Quilt Size
6"	13 x 15	195	418	224	92" x 106"
7"	11 x 13	143	310	168	89" x 105"
8"	10 x 12	120	262	143	91" x 109"

1½" Sashing

Block Size	Block Layout	No. of Blocks	No. of Sashing Strips	No. of Sashing Squares	Quilt Size
6"	12 x 14	168	362	195	91½" x 106½"
7"	10 x 12	120	262	143	86½" x 103½"
8"	9 x 11	99	218	120	87" x 106"
9"	9 x 10	90	199	110	96" x 106½"
10"	8 x 9	72	161	90	93½" x 105"

2" Sashing

Block Size	Block Layout	No. of Blocks	No. of Sashing Strips	No. of Sashing Squares	Quilt Size
6"	11 x 13	143	310	168	90" x 106"
7"	10 x 11	110	241	132	92" x 101"
8"	9 x 10	90	199	110	92" x 102"
9"	8 x 9	72	161	90	90" x 101"
10"	7 x 8	56	127	72	86" x 98"
11"	7 x 8	56	127	72	93" x 106"
12"	6 x 7	42	97	56	86" x 100"

2½" Sashing

Block Size	Block Layout	No. of Blocks	No. of Sashing Strips	No. of Sashing Squares	Quilt Size
6"	10 x 12	120	262	143	87½" x 104½"
7"	9 x 11	99	218	120	88" x 107"
8"	8 x 10	80	178	99	86½" x 107½"
9"	8 x 9	72	161	90	94½" x 106"
10"	7 x 8	56	127	72	90" x 102½"
11"	6 x 7	42	97	56	83½" x 97"
12"	6 x 7	42	97	56	89½" x 104"
13"	5 x 6	30	71	42	80" x 95½"

3" Sashing

Block Size	Block Layout	No. of Blocks	No. of Sashing Strips	No. of Sashing Squares	Quilt Size
7"	9 x 10	90	199	110	93" x 103"
8"	8 x 10	80	178	99	91" x 113"
9"	7 x 9	63	142	80	87" x 111"
10"	7 x 8	56	127	72	94" x 107"
11"	6 x 7	42	97	56	87" x 101"
12"	6 x 7	42	97	56	93" x 108"
13"	5 x 6	30	71	42	83" x 99"
14"	5 x 6	30	71	42	88" x 105"

King Sizes (Without Borders)

1" Sashing

Block Size	Block Layout	No. of Blocks	No. of Sashing Strips	No. of Sashing Squares	Quilt Size
5"	18 x 18	324	684	361	109" x 109"
6"	15 x 15	225	480	256	106" x 106"
7"	13 x 13	169	364	196	105" x 105"
8"	11 x 11	121	264	144	100" x 100"

1½" Sashing

Block Size	Block Layout	No. of Blocks	No. of Sashing Strips	No. of Sashing Squares	Quilt Size
5"	16 x 16	256	544	289	105½" x 105½"
6"	14 x 14	196	420	225	106½" x 106½"
7"	12 x 12	144	312	169	103½" x 103½"
8"	11 x 11	121	264	144	106" x 106"
9"	10 x 10	100	220	121	106½" x 106½"
10"	9 x 9	81	180	100	105" x 105"

2" Sashing

Block Size	Block Layout	No. of Blocks	No. of Sashing Strips	No. of Sashing Squares	Quilt Size
5"	15 x 15	225	480	256	107" x 107
6"	13 x 13	169	364	196	106" x 106"
7"	11 x 11	121	264	144	101" x 101"
8"	10 x 10	100	220	121	102" x 102"
9"	9 x 9	81	180	100	101" x 101"
10"	9 x 9	81	180	100	110" x 110"
11"	8 x 8	64	144	81	106" x 106"
12"	7 x 7	49	112	64	100" x 100"

2½" Sashing

Block Size	Block Layout	No. of Blocks	No. of Sashing Strips	No. of Sashing Squares	Quilt Size
6"	12 x 12	144	312	169	104½" x 104½"
7"	11 x 11	121	264	144	107" x 107"
8"	10 x 10	100	220	121	107½" x 107½"
9"	9 x 9	81	180	100	106" x 106"
10"	8 x 8	64	144	81	102½" x 102½"
11"	7 x 7	49	112	64	97" x 97"
12"	7 x 7	49	112	64	104" x 104"

3" Sashing

Block Size	Block Layout	No. of Blocks	No. of Sashing Strips	No. of Sashing Squares	Quilt Size
6"	11 x 11	121	264	144	102" x 102"
7"	10 x 10	100	220	121	103" x 103"
8"	9 x 9	81	180	100	102" x 102"
9"	8 x 8	64	144	81	99" x 99"
10"	8 x 8	64	144	81	107" x 107"
11"	7 x 7	49	112	64	101" x 101"
12"	7 x 7	49	112	64	108" x 108"
13"	6 x 6	36	84	49	99" x 99"

Straight Set With Alternating Squares

Crib Sizes (Without Borders)

Block Size	Block Layout	No. of Blocks	No. of Squares	Quilt Size
4"	7 x 11	39	38	28" x 44"
5"	5 x 9	23	22	25" x 45"
6"	5 x 7	18	17	30" x 42"
7"	5 x 7	18	17	35" x 49"
8"	3 x 5	8	7	24" x 40"

Twin Sizes (Without Borders)

Block Size	Block Layout	No. of Blocks	No. of Squares	Quilt Size
5"	13 x 19	124	123	65" x 95"
6"	11 x 17	94	93	66" x 102
7"	9 x 15	68	67	63" x 105"
8"	9 x 13	59	58	72" x 104"
9"	7 x 11	39	38	63" x 99"
10"	7 x 9	32	31	70" x 90"
11"	7 x 9	32	31	77" x 99"
12"	5 x 7	18	17	60" x 84"
13"	5 x 7	18	17	65" x 91"
14"	5 x 7	18	17	70" x 98"

Full Sizes (Without Borders)

Block Size	Block Layout	No. of Blocks	No. of Squares	Quilt Size
5"	15 x 19	143	142	75" x 95"
6"	13 x 15	98	97	78" x 90"
7"	11 x 13	72	71	77" x 91"
8"	11 x 13	72	71	88" x 104"
9"	9 x 11	50	49	81" x 99"

Full Sizes (Without Borders)

Block Size	Block Layout	No. of Blocks	No. of Squares	Quilt Size
10"	9 x 11	50	49	90" x 110"
11"	7 x 9	32	31	77" x 99"
12"	7 x 9	32	31	84" x 108"
13"	5 x 7	18	17	65" x 91"
14"	5 x 7	18	17	70" x 98"

Queen Sizes (Without Borders)

Block Size	Block Layout	No. of Blocks	No. of Squares	Quilt Size
5"	19 x 21	200	199	90" x 105"
6"	15 x 17	128	127	90" x 102"
7"	13 x 15	98	97	91" x 105"
8"	11 x 13	72	71	88" x 104"
9"	9 x 11	50	49	81" x 99"
10"	9 x 9	41	40	90" x 90"
11"	7 x 9	32	31	77" x 99"
12"	7 x 9	32	31	84" x 108"
13"	7 x 7	25	24	91" x 91"
14"	7 x 7	25	24	98" x 98"
15"	5 x 7	18	17	75" x 105"
16"	5 x 5	13	12	80" x 80"
17"	5 x 5	13	12	85" x 85"
18"	5 x 5	13	12	90" x 90"

King Sizes (Without Borders)

Block Size	Block Layout	No. of Blocks	No. of Squares	Quilt Size
5"	21 x 21	221	220	105" x 105"
6"	17 x 17	145	144	102" x 102"
7"	15 x 15	113	112	105" x 105"
8"	13 x 13	85	84	104" x 104"
9"	11 x 11	61	60	99" x 99"
10"	11 x 11	61	60	110" x 110"
11"	9 x 9	41	40	99" x 99"
12"	9 x 9	41	40	108" x 108"
13"	7 x 7	25	24	91" x 91"
14"	7 x 7	25	24	98" x 98"
15"	7 x 7	25	24	105" x 105"
16"	7 x 7	25	24	112" x 112"
17"	5 x 5	13	12	85" x 85"
18"	5 x 5	13	12	90" x 90"
19"	5 x 5	13	12	95" x 95"
20"	5 x 5	13	12	100" x 100"
21"	5 x 5	13	12	105" x 105"

Diagonal Set

Note: *For the diagonal sets listed in the charts below, the block layout given is the largest dimension of rows point to point. More blocks are filled in between the rows to complete the layout. Final measurements are rounded to the nearest eighth.*

Twin Sizes (Without Borders)

Block Size	Diagonal Size	Block Layout	No. of Blocks	No. of Setting Triangles	Quilt Size
4"	5⅝"	11 x 17	347	52	61⅞" x 95⅝"
5"	7"	9 x 14	230	42	63" x 98"
6"	8½"	8 x 12	173	36	68" x 102"
7"	9⅞"	6 x 10	105	28	59¼" x 98¾"
8"	11⁵⁄₁₆"	6 x 9	94	26	67⅞" x 101¾"
9"	12¾"	5 x 8	68	22	63¾" x 102"
10"	14⅛"	5 x 7	59	20	70⅝" x 98⅞"
11"	15½"	4 x 6	39	16	62" x 93"

Full Sizes (Without Borders)

Block Size	Diagonal Size	Block Layout	No. of Blocks	No. of Setting Triangles	Quilt Size
5"	7"	12 x 14	311	48	84" x 98"
6"	8½"	10 x 12	219	40	85" x 102"
7"	9⅞"	8 x 10	143	32	79" x 98¾"
8"	11⁵⁄₁₆"	7 x 9	111	28	79⅛" x 101¾"
9"	12¾"	6 x 8	83	24	76½" x 102"

Full Sizes (Without Borders)

Block Size	Diagonal Size	Block Layout	No. of Blocks	No. of Setting Triangles	Quilt Size
10"	14⅛"	6 x 7	72	22	84¾" x 98⅞"
11"	15½"	5 x 6	50	18	77½" x 93"
12"	17"	5 x 6	50	18	85" x 102"

Queen Sizes (Without Borders)

Block Size	Diagonal Size	Block Layout	No. of Blocks	No. of Setting Triangles	Quilt Size
5"	7"	13 x 15	363	52	91" x 105"
6"	8½"	10 x 12	219	40	85" x 102"
7"	9⅞"	9 x 10	162	34	88⅞" x 98¾"
8"	11⁵⁄₁₆"	8 x 9	128	30	90½" x 101¾"
9"	12¾"	7 x 8	98	26	89¼" x 102"
10"	14⅛"	6 x 7	72	22	84¾" x 98⅞"
11"	15½"	6 x 7	72	22	93" x 108½"
12"	17"	5 x 6	50	18	85" x 102"
13"	18⅜"	5 x 6	50	18	91⅞" x 110¼"
14"	19¾"	4 x 5	32	14	79" x 98¾"
15"	21⅛"	4 x 5	32	14	84½" x 105⅝"

King Sizes (Without Borders)

Block Size	Diagonal Size	Block Layout	No. of Blocks	No. of Setting Triangles	Quilt Size
5"	7"	15 x 15	421	56	105" x 105"
6"	8½"	12 x 12	265	44	102" x 102"
7"	9⅞"	10 x 10	181	36	98¾" x 98¾"
8"	11⁵⁄₁₆"	9 x 9	145	32	101¾" x 101¾"
9"	12¾"	8 x 8	113	28	102" x 102"
10"	14⅛"	8 x 8	113	28	113" x 113"
11"	15½"	7 x 7	85	24	108½" x 108½"
12"	17"	6 x 6	61	20	102" x 102"
13"	18⅜"	6 x 6	61	20	110¼" x 110¼"
14"	19¾"	5 x 5	41	16	98¾" x 98¾"
15"	21⅛"	5 x 5	41	16	105⅝" x 105⅝"
16"	22⅝"	5 x 5	41	16	113⅛" x 113⅛"
17"	24"	4 x 4	25	12	96" x 96"

Note: *To figure yardage for setting triangles, use diagonal size (which is finished size), and refer to the* ***Figuring Yardage*** *chart for* ***Quarter-Square Triangles*** *on pages 32–34. Don't forget to include two squares the finished-block size (column 1) for corner triangles in your yardage amount.*

Diagonal Set With Sashing

Twin Sizes (Without Borders)

1" Sashing (diagonal width, 1⅜")

Block Size	Diagonal Size	Block Layout	No. of Blocks	No. of Sashing Strips	No. of Sashing Squares	No. of Setting Triangles	Quilt Size
4"	5⅝"	9 x 14	230	504	275	42	64⅜" x 99⅜"
5"	7"	8 x 12	173	384	212	36	68⅜" x 101⅜"
6"	8½"	6 x 10	105	240	136	28	60⅝" x 100⅛"
7"	9⅞"	6 x 9	94	216	123	26	68⅞" x 102⅝"

1½" Sashing (diagonal width, 2⅛")

Block Size	Diagonal Size	Block Layout	No. of Blocks	No. of Sashing Strips	No. of Sashing Squares	No. of Setting Triangles	Quilt Size
5"	7"	7 x 11	137	308	172	32	66" x 102½"
6"	8½"	6 x 9	94	216	123	26	65⅞" x 97¾"
7"	9⅞"	5 x 8	68	160	93	22	62⅛" x 98⅛"
8"	11⁵⁄₁₆"	5 x 7	59	140	82	20	69¼" x 96⅛"
9"	12¾"	4 x 7	46	112	67	18	61⅝" x 106¼"

2" Sashing (diagonal width, 2¾")

Block Size	Diagonal Size	Block Layout	No. of Blocks	No. of Sashing Strips	No. of Sashing Squares	No. of Setting Triangles	Quilt Size
5"	7"	6 x 10	105	240	136	28	61¼" x 101¼"
6"	8½"	6 x 9	94	216	123	26	70¼" x 104"
7"	9⅞"	5 x 8	68	160	93	22	65⅞" x 103¾"
8"	11⁵⁄₁₆"	4 x 7	46	112	67	18	59" x 100¼"
9"	12¾"	4 x 6	39	96	58	16	64¾" x 95¾"
10"	14⅛"	4 x 6	39	96	58	16	70¼" x 104"

2½" Sashing (diagonal width, 3½")

Block Size	Diagonal Size	Block Layout	No. of Blocks	No. of Sashing Strips	No. of Sashing Squares	No. of Setting Triangles	Quilt Size
6"	8½"	5 x 8	68	160	93	22	63½" x 99½"
7"	9⅞"	5 x 7	59	140	82	20	70⅜" x 97⅛"
8"	11⁵⁄₁₆"	4 x 7	46	112	67	18	62½" x 106¾"
9"	12¾"	4 x 6	39	96	58	16	68½" x 101"

Twin Sizes (Without Borders)

3" Sashing (diagonal width, 4¼")

Block Size	Diagonal Size	Block Layout	No. of Blocks	No. of Sashing Strips	No. of Sashing Squares	No. of Setting Triangles	Quilt Size
6"	8½"	5 x 8	68	160	93	22	68" x 106¼"
7"	9⅞"	4 x 7	46	112	67	18	60¾" x 103⅛"
8"	11⁵⁄₁₆"	4 x 6	39	96	58	16	66½" x 97⅝"
9"	12¾"	4 x 6	39	96	58	16	72¼" x 106¼"

Full Sizes (Without Borders)

1" Sashing (diagonal width, 1⅜")

Block Size	Diagonal Size	Block Layout	No. of Blocks	No. of Sashing Strips	No. of Sashing Squares	No. of Setting Triangles	Quilt Size
5"	7"	10 x 12	219	480	262	40	85⅛" x 101⅞"
6"	8½"	8 x 10	143	320	178	32	80⅜" x 100¼"
7"	9⅞"	7 x 9	111	252	142	28	80⅛" x 102⅝"
8"	11⁵⁄₁₆"	7 x 8	98	224	127	26	90¼" x 102⅞"

1½" Sashing (diagonal width, 2⅛")

Block Size	Diagonal Size	Block Layout	No. of Blocks	No. of Sashing Strips	No. of Sashing Squares	No. of Setting Triangles	Quilt Size
5"	7"	9 x 11	179	396	218	36	84¼" x 102½"
6"	8½"	8 x 10	143	320	178	32	87⅛" x 108⅜"
7"	9⅞"	7 x 9	111	252	142	28	86⅛" x 110⅛"
8"	11⁵⁄₁₆"	6 x 8	83	192	110	24	82¾" x 109⅝"
9"	12¾"	6 x 7	72	168	97	22	91⅜" x 106¼"

2" Sashing (diagonal width, 2¾")

Block Size	Diagonal Size	Block Layout	No. of Blocks	No. of Sashing Strips	No. of Sashing Squares	No. of Setting Triangles	Quilt Size
5"	7"	8 x 10	143	320	178	32	80¾" x 100¼"
6"	8½"	7 x 9	111	252	142	28	81½" x 104"
7"	9⅞"	6 x 8	83	192	110	24	78½" x 103¾"
8"	11⁵⁄₁₆"	6 x 7	72	168	97	22	87⅛" x 101¼"
9"	12¾"	5 x 7	59	140	82	20	80¼" x 111¼"
10"	14⅛"	5 x 6	50	120	71	18	87⅛" x 104"

2½" Sashing (diagonal width, 3½")

Block Size	Diagonal Size	Block Layout	No. of Blocks	No. of Sashing Strips	No. of Sashing Squares	No. of Setting Triangles	Quilt Size
5"	7"	7 x 9	111	252	142	28	77" x 98"
6"	8½"	7 x 8	98	224	127	26	87½" x 99½"
7"	9⅞"	6 x 8	83	192	110	24	83¾" x 110½"
8"	11⁵⁄₁₆"	6 x 7	72	168	97	22	92⅜" x 107¼"
9"	12¾"	5 x 6	50	120	71	18	84¾" x 101"
10"	14⅛"	5 x 6	50	120	71	18	91⅝" x 109¼"
11"	15½"	4 x 5	32	80	49	14	79½" x 98½"
12"	17"	4 x 5	32	80	49	14	85½" x 106"

Full Sizes (Without Borders)

3" Sashing (diagonal width, 4¼")

Block Size	Diagonal Size	Block Layout	No. of Blocks	No. of Sashing Strips	No. of Sashing Squares	No. of Setting Triangles	Quilt Size
6"	8½"	6 x 8	83	192	110	24	80¾" x 106¼"
7"	9⅞"	6 x 7	72	168	97	22	89" x 103⅛"
8"	11⁵⁄₁₆"	5 x 6	50	120	71	18	82" x 97⅝"
9"	12¾"	5 x 6	50	120	71	18	89¼" x 106¼"
10"	14⅛"	4 x 5	32	80	49	14	77¾" x 96⅛"
11"	15½"	4 x 5	32	80	49	14	83¼" x 103"
12"	17"	4 x 5	32	80	49	14	89¼" x 110½"

Queen Sizes (Without Borders)

1" Sashing (diagonal width, 1⅜")

Block Size	Diagonal Size	Block Layout	No. of Blocks	No. of Sashing Strips	No. of Sashing Squares	No. of Setting Triangles	Quilt Size
4"	5⅝"	13 x 15	363	780	418	52	92⅜" x 106⅜"
5"	7"	11 x 13	263	572	310	44	93½" x 110¼"
6"	8½"	9 x 11	179	396	218	36	90¼" x 110"
7"	9⅞"	8 x 9	128	288	161	30	91⅜" x 102⅝"
8"	11⁵⁄₁₆"	7 x 8	98	224	127	26	90⅛" x 102⅞"

1½" Sashing (diagonal width, 2⅛")

Block Size	Diagonal Size	Block Layout	No. of Blocks	No. of Sashing Strips	No. of Sashing Squares	No. of Setting Triangles	Quilt Size
5"	7"	10 x 11	200	440	241	38	93⅜" x 102½"
6"	8½"	8 x 10	143	320	178	32	87⅛" x 108⅜"
7"	9⅞"	7 x 9	111	252	142	28	86⅛" x 110⅛"
8"	11⁵⁄₁₆"	7 x 8	98	224	127	26	96⅛" x 109⅝"
9"	12¾"	6 x 7	72	168	97	22	91⅜" x 106¼"

2" Sashing (diagonal width, 2¾")

Block Size	Diagonal Size	Block Layout	No. of Blocks	No. of Sashing Strips	No. of Sashing Squares	No. of Setting Triangles	Quilt Size
5"	7"	9 x 10	162	360	199	34	90½" x 100¼"
6"	8½"	8 x 9	128	288	161	30	92¾" x 104"
7"	9⅞"	7 x 8	98	224	127	26	91⅛" x 103¾"
8"	11⁵⁄₁₆"	6 x 7	72	168	97	22	87⅛" x 101⅛"
9"	12¾"	6 x 7	72	168	97	22	95¾" x 111¼"
10"	14⅛"	5 x 6	50	120	71	18	87⅛" x 104"

Queen Sizes (Without Borders)

2½" Sashing (diagonal width, 3½")

Block Size	Diagonal Size	Block Layout	No. of Blocks	No. of Sashing Strips	No. of Sashing Squares	No. of Setting Triangles	Quilt Size
5"	7"	8 x 9	128	288	161	30	87½" x 98"
6"	8½"	7 x 8	98	224	127	26	87½" x 99½"
7"	9⅞"	6 x 7	72	168	97	22	83¾" x 97⅛"
8"	11⁵⁄₁₆"	6 x 7	72	168	97	22	92⅜" x 107⅛"
9"	12¾"	5 x 6	50	120	71	18	84¾" x 101"
10"	14⅛"	5 x 6	50	120	71	18	91⅝" x 109¼"

3" Sashing (diagonal width, 4¼")

Block Size	Diagonal Size	Block Layout	No. of Blocks	No. of Sashing Strips	No. of Sashing Squares	No. of Setting Triangles	Quilt Size
6"	8½"	7 x 8	98	224	127	26	93½" x 106¼"
7"	9⅞"	6 x 7	72	168	97	22	89" x 103⅛"
8"	11⁵⁄₁₆"	6 x 7	72	168	97	22	97⅝" x 113¼"
9"	12¾"	5 x 6	50	120	71	18	89¼" x 106¼"
10"	14⅛"	5 x 6	50	120	71	18	96⅛" x 114½"
11"	15½"	4 x 5	32	80	49	14	83¼" x 103"
12"	17"	4 x 5	32	80	49	14	89¼" x 110½"

King Sizes (Without Borders)

1" Sashing (diagonal width, 1⅜")

Block Size	Diagonal Size	Block Layout	No. of Blocks	No. of Sashing Strips	No. of Sashing Squares	No. of Setting Triangles	Quilt Size
4"	5⅝"	15 x 15	421	900	480	56	106⅜" x 106⅜"
5"	7"	13 x 13	313	676	364	48	110¼" x 110¼"
6"	8½"	11 x 11	221	484	264	40	110" x 110"
7"	9⅞"	9 x 9	145	324	180	32	102⅝" x 102⅝"
8"	11⁵⁄₁₆"	8 x 8	113	256	144	28	102⅞" x 102⅞"

1½" Sashing (diagonal width, 2⅛")

Block Size	Diagonal Size	Block Layout	No. of Blocks	No. of Sashing Strips	No. of Sashing Squares	No. of Setting Triangles	Quilt Size
4"	5⅝"	13 x 13	313	676	364	48	102⅞" x 102⅞"
5"	7"	11 x 11	221	484	264	40	102½" x 102½"
6"	8½"	9 x 9	145	324	180	32	97¾" x 97¾"
7"	9⅞"	8 x 8	113	256	144	28	98⅛" x 98⅛"
8"	11⁵⁄₁₆"	8 x 8	113	256	144	28	109⅝" x 109⅝"
9"	12¾"	7 x 7	85	196	112	24	106¼" x 106¼"

King Sizes (Without Borders)

2" Sashing (diagonal width, 2¾")

Block Size	Diagonal Size	Block Layout	No. of Blocks	No. of Sashing Strips	No. of Sashing Squares	No. of Setting Triangles	Quilt Size
5"	7"	11 x 11	221	484	264	40	110" x 110"
6"	8½"	9 x 9	145	324	180	32	104" x 104"
7"	9⅞"	8 x 8	113	256	144	28	103¾" x 103¾"
8"	11⁵⁄₁₆"	7 x 7	85	196	112	24	101⅛" x 101⅛"
9"	12¾"	7 x 7	85	196	112	24	111¼" x 111¼"
10"	14⅛"	6 x 6	61	144	84	20	104" x 104"

2½" Sashing (diagonal width, 3½")

Block Size	Diagonal Size	Block Layout	No. of Blocks	No. of Sashing Strips	No. of Sashing Squares	No. of Setting Triangles	Quilt Size
5"	7"	10 x 10	181	400	220	36	108½" x 108½"
6"	8½"	9 x 9	145	324	180	32	111½" x 111½"
7"	9⅞"	8 x 8	113	256	144	28	110½" x 110½"
8"	11⁵⁄₁₆"	7 x 7	85	196	112	24	107⅛" x 107⅛"
9"	12¾"	6 x 6	61	144	84	20	101" x 101"
10"	14⅛"	6 x 6	61	144	84	20	109¼" x 109¼"
11"	15½"	5 x 5	41	100	60	16	98½" x 98½"
12"	17"	5 x 5	41	100	60	16	106" x 106"

3" Sashing (diagonal width, 4¼")

Block Size	Diagonal Size	Block Layout	No. of Blocks	No. of Sashing Strips	No. of Sashing Squares	No. of Setting Triangles	Quilt Size
5"	7"	9 x 9	145	324	180	32	105½" x 105½"
6"	8½"	8 x 8	113	256	144	28	106¼" x 106¼"
7"	9⅞"	7 x 7	85	196	112	24	103⅛" x 103⅛"
8"	11⁵⁄₁₆"	6 x 6	61	144	84	20	97⅝" x 97⅝"
9"	12¾"	6 x 6	61	144	84	20	106¼" x 106¼"
10"	14⅛"	5 x 5	41	100	60	16	96⅛" x 96⅛"
11"	15½"	5 x 5	41	100	60	16	103" x 103"
12"	17"	5 x 5	41	100	60	16	110½" x 110½"

***Note:** To figure yardage for setting triangles, use the diagonal size of block plus sashing. For example, if the block is 6" and sashing is 1½", use 7½" as the "new" block measurement. Refer to **Diagonal Measurement of Blocks** chart on page 41 for the diagonal measurement, then refer to the **Figuring Yardage** chart for **Quarter-Square Triangles**, pages 32–34 to figure yardage. Don't forget to add to the yardage amount: two squares the finished-block size plus the sashing width (column 1) for corner triangles.*

Diagonal Set With Alternating Squares

Twin Sizes (Without Borders)

Block Size	Diagonal Size	Block Layout	No. of Blocks	No. of Squares	No. of Setting Triangles	Quilt Size
4"	5⅝"	11 x 17	187	160	52	61⅞" x 95⅝"
5"	7"	9 x 14	126	104	42	63" x 98"
6"	8½"	8 x 12	96	77	36	68" x 102"
7"	9⅞"	6 x 10	60	45	28	59¼" x 98¾"
8"	11 5/16"	6 x 9	54	40	26	67⅞" x 101¾"
9"	12¾"	5 x 8	40	28	22	63¾" x 102"
10"	14⅛"	5 x 7	35	24	20	70⅝" x 98⅞"
11"	15½"	4 x 6	24	15	16	62" x 93"

Full Sizes (Without Borders)

Block Size	Diagonal Size	Block Layout	No. of Blocks	No. of Squares	No. of Setting Triangles	Quilt Size
5"	7"	12 x 14	168	143	48	84" x 98"
6"	8½"	10 x 12	120	99	40	85" x 102"
7"	9⅞"	8 x 10	80	63	32	79" x 98¾"
8"	11 5/16"	7 x 9	63	48	28	79⅛" x 101¾"
9"	12¾"	6 x 8	48	35	24	76½" x 102"
10"	14⅛"	6 x 7	42	30	22	84¾" x 98⅞"
11"	15½"	5 x 6	30	20	18	77½" x 93"
12"	17"	5 x 6	30	20	18	85" x 102"

Queen Sizes (Without Borders)

Block Size	Diagonal Size	Block Layout	No. of Blocks	No. of Squares	No. of Setting Triangles	Quilt Size
5"	7"	13 x 15	195	168	52	91" x 105"
6"	8½"	10 x 12	120	99	40	80½" x 102"
7"	9⅞"	9 x 10	90	72	34	88⅞" x 98¾"
8"	115⁄16"	8 x 9	72	56	30	90½" x 101¾"
9"	12¾"	7 x 8	56	42	26	89¼" x 102"
10"	14⅛"	6 x 7	42	30	22	84¾" x 98⅞"
11"	15½"	6 x 7	42	30	22	93" x 108½"
12"	17"	5 x 6	30	20	18	85" x 102"
13"	18⅜"	5 x 6	30	20	18	91⅞" x 110¼"

King Sizes (Without Borders)

Block Size	Diagonal Size	Block Layout	No. of Blocks	No. of Squares	No. of Setting Triangles	Quilt Size
5"	7"	15 x 15	225	196	56	105" x 105"
6"	8½"	12 x 12	144	121	44	102" x 102"
7"	9⅞"	10 x 10	100	81	36	98¾" x 98¾"
8"	115⁄16"	9 x 9	81	64	32	101¾" x 101¾"
9"	12¾"	8 x 8	64	49	28	102" x 102"
10"	14⅛"	8 x 8	64	49	28	113" x 113"
11"	15½"	7 x 7	49	36	24	108½" x 108½"
12"	17"	6 x 6	36	25	20	102" x 102"
13"	18⅜"	6 x 6	36	25	20	110¼" x 110¼"
14"	19¾"	5 x 5	25	16	16	98¾" x 98¾"
15"	21⅛"	5 x 5	25	16	16	105⅝" x 105⅝"
16"	22⅝"	5 x 5	25	16	16	113⅛" x 113⅛"
17"	24"	4 x 4	16	9	12	96" x 96"

Note: *To figure yardage for setting triangles, use diagonal size (which is finished size) and refer to* ***Figuring Yardage*** *for* ***Quarter-Square Triangles****, pages 32–34. Don't forget to add to the yardage: two squares the finished-block size (column 1) for corner triangles.*

Figuring Yardage

Rectangles

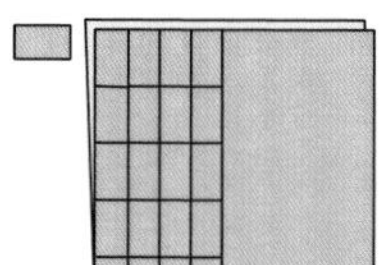

Cutting Note: *This cutting layout shows the most efficient use of fabric. If using a rotary cutter (mat and ruler), cut strips the correct width, and then cut rectangles. For templates, be sure to butt up the edges as in the drawing; trace and cut.*

Rectangles From Yardage

Finished Size	Cut Size	Approximate No. of Rectangles From Yardage											
		¼ yd	½ yd	¾ yd	1 yd	1¼ yds	1½ yds	1¾ yds	2 yds	2¼ yds	2½ yds	2¾ yds	3 yds
1" x 2"	**1½" x 2½"**	96	192	288	384	480	576	672	768	864	960	1056	1152
1" x 2½"	**1½" x 3"**	78	156	234	312	390	468	546	624	702	780	858	936
1" x 3"	**1½" x 3½"**	66	132	198	264	330	396	462	528	594	660	726	792
1" x 3½"	**1½" x 4"**	60	120	180	240	300	360	420	480	540	600	660	720
1" x 4"	**1½" x 4½"**	48	96	144	192	240	288	336	384	432	480	528	576
1" x 4½"	**1½" x 5"**	48	96	144	192	240	288	336	384	432	480	528	576
1" x 5"	**1½" x 5½"**	42	84	126	168	210	252	294	336	378	420	462	504
1" x 5½"	**1½" x 6"**	36	72	108	144	180	216	252	288	324	360	396	432
1" x 6"	**1½" x 6½"**	36	72	108	144	180	216	252	288	324	360	396	432
1½" x 2"	**2" x 2½"**	64	144	208	288	352	432	496	576	640	720	784	864
1½" x 2½"	**2" x 3"**	52	117	169	234	286	351	403	468	520	585	637	702
1½" x 3"	**2" x 3½"**	44	99	143	198	242	297	341	396	440	495	539	594
1½" x 3½"	**2" x 4"**	40	90	130	180	220	270	310	360	400	450	490	540
1½" x 4"	**2" x 4½"**	32	72	104	144	176	216	248	288	320	360	392	432
1½" x 4½"	**2" x 5"**	32	72	104	144	176	216	248	288	320	360	392	432
1½" x 5"	**2" x 5½"**	28	63	91	126	154	189	217	252	280	315	343	378
1½" x 5½"	**2" x 6"**	24	54	78	108	132	162	186	216	240	270	294	324
1½" x 6"	**2" x 6½"**	24	54	78	108	132	162	186	216	240	270	294	324

Rectangles From Yardage

Finished Size	Cut Size	Approximate No. of Rectangles From Yardage											
		¼ yd	½ yd	¾ yd	1 yd	1¼ yds	1½ yds	1¾ yds	2 yds	2¼ yds	2½ yds	2¾ yds	3 yds
2" x 3"	**2½" x 3½"**	33	77	110	154	198	231	275	308	352	396	429	473
2" x 3½"	**2½" x 4"**	30	70	100	140	180	210	250	280	320	360	390	430
2" x 4"	**2½" x 4½"**	24	56	80	112	144	168	200	224	256	288	312	344
2" x 4½"	**2½" x 5"**	24	56	80	112	144	168	200	224	256	288	312	344
2" x 5"	**2½" x 5½"**	21	49	70	98	126	147	175	196	224	252	273	301
2" x 5½"	**2½" x 6"**	18	42	60	84	108	126	150	168	192	216	234	258
2" x 6"	**2 ½" x 6½"**	18	42	60	84	108	126	150	168	192	216	234	258
2½" x 3"	**3" x 3½"**	33	66	99	144	165	198	231	264	297	330	363	396
2½" x 3½"	**3" x 4"**	30	60	90	120	150	180	210	240	270	300	330	360
2½" x 4"	**3" x 4½"**	24	48	72	96	120	144	168	192	216	248	264	288
2½" x 4½"	**3" x 5"**	24	48	72	96	120	144	168	192	216	248	264	288
2½" x 5"	**3" x 5½"**	21	42	63	84	105	126	147	168	189	210	231	252
2½" x 5½"	**3" x 6"**	18	36	54	72	90	108	126	144	162	180	198	216
2½" x 6"	**3" x 6½"**	18	36	54	72	90	108	126	144	162	180	198	216
3" x 4"	**3½" x 4½"**	16	40	56	80	96	120	144	160	184	200	224	240
3" x 4½"	**3½" x 5"**	16	40	56	80	96	120	144	160	184	200	224	240
3" x 5"	**3½" x 5½"**	14	35	49	70	84	105	126	140	161	175	196	210
3" x 5½"	**3½" x 6"**	12	30	42	60	72	90	108	120	138	150	168	180
3" x 6"	**3½" x 6½"**	12	30	42	60	72	90	108	120	138	150	168	180
4" x 5"	**4½" x 5½"**	14	28	42	56	70	84	98	112	126	140	154	168
4" x 5½"	**4½" x 6"**	12	24	36	48	60	72	84	96	108	120	132	144
4" x 6"	**4½" x 6½"**	12	24	36	48	60	72	84	96	108	120	132	144
5" x 6"	**5½" x 6½"**	6	18	24	36	48	54	66	78	84	96	108	114

For larger sizes of rectangles, see Sashing Strips on page 35.

Rectangles From Precuts

Finished Size	Cut Size	Approximate No. of Rectangles From Precuts*						
		1½" x 42"	2½" x 42"	5" x 42"	5" x 5"	10" x 10"	16" x 16"	18" x 21"
1" x 2"	**1½" x 2½"**	16	16	48	6	24	60	96
1" x 2½"	**1½" x 3"**	14	14	42	3	18	50	84
1" x 3"	**1½" x 3½"**	12	12	36	3	12	40	72
1" x 3½"	**1½" x 4"**	10	10	30	3	12	40	60
1" x 4"	**1½" x 4½"**	9	9	27	3	12	30	48
1" x 4½"	**1½" x 5"**	8	8	24	3	12	30	48
1" x 5"	**1½" x 5½"**	7	7	21		6	20	36
1" x 5½"	**1½" x 6"**	7	7	21		6	20	36
1" x 6"	**1½" x 6½"**	6	6	18		6	20	36
1½" x 2"	**2" x 2½"**		16	32	4	20	48	72
1½" x 2½"	**2" x 3"**		14	28	2	15	40	63
1½" x 3"	**2" x 3½"**		12	24	2	10	32	54
1½" x 3½"	**2" x 4"**		10	20	2	10	32	45
1½" x 4"	**2" x 4½"**		9	18	2	10	24	36
1½" x 4½"	**2" x 5"**		8	16	2	10	24	36
1½" x 5"	**2" x 5½"**		7	14		5	16	27
1½" x 5½"	**2" x 6"**		7	14		5	16	27
1½" x 6"	**2" x 6½"**		6	12		5	16	27
2" x 3"	**2½" x 3½"**		12	24	2	8	24	42
2" x 3½"	**2½" x 4"**		10	20	2	8	24	35
2" x 4"	**2½" x 4½"**		9	18	2	8	18	28
2" x 4½"	**2½" x 5"**		8	16	2	8	18	28
2" x 5"	**2½" x 5½"**		7	14		4	12	21
2" x 5½"	**2½" x 6"**		7	14		4	12	21
2" x 6"	**2 ½" x 6½"**		6	12		4	12	21
2½" x 3"	**3" x 3½"**			12	1	6	20	36
2½" x 3½"	**3" x 4"**			10	1	6	20	30
2½" x 4"	**3" x 4½"**			9	1	6	15	24
2½" x 4½"	**3" x 5"**			8	1	6	15	24
2½" x 5"	**3" x 5½"**			7		3	10	18
2½" x 5½"	**3" x 6"**			7		3	10	18
2½" x 6"	**3" x 6½"**			6		3	10	18
3" x 4"	**3½" x 4½"**			9	1	4	12	20
3" x 4½"	**3½" x 5"**			8	1	4	12	20
3" x 5"	**3½" x 5½"**			7		2	8	15
3" x 5½"	**3½" x 6"**			7		2	8	15
3" x 6"	**3½" x 6½"**			6		2	8	15
4" x 5"	**4½" x 5½"**			7		2	6	12
4" x 5½"	**4½" x 6"**			7		2	6	12
4" x 6"	**4½" x 6½"**			6		2	6	12
5" x 6"	**5½" x 6½"**					1	4	9

*For more information about precuts, see page 2.

Squares

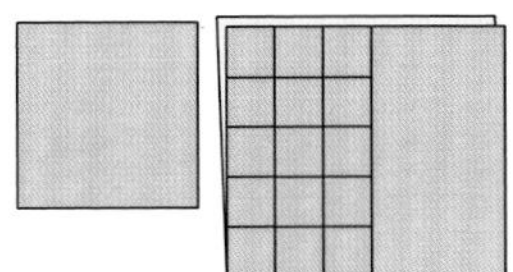

Cutting Note: *This cutting layout shows the most efficient use of fabric. If using a rotary cutter (mat and ruler), cut strips the correct width, and then cut squares. For templates, be sure to butt up the edges as in the drawing; trace and cut.*

Squares From Yardage

Finished Size	Cut Size	Approximate No. of Squares from Yardage																			
		¼ yd	½ yd	¾ yd	1 yd	1¼ yds	1½ yds	1¾ yds	2 yds	2¼ yds	2½ yds	2¾ yds	3 yds	3¼ yds	3½ yds	3¾ yds	4 yds	4¼ yds	4½ yds	4¾ yds	5 yds
1"	**1½"**	156	312	468	624	780	936	1092	1248	1404	1560	1716	1872	2028	2184	2340	2496	2652	2808	2964	3120
1¼"	**1¾"**	110	220	330	440	550	660	792	902	1012	1122	1232	1342	1452	1584	1694	1804	1914	2024	2134	2244
1½"	**2"**	80	180	260	360	440	540	620	720	800	900	980	1080	1160	1260	1340	1440	1520	1620	1700	1800
1¾"	**2¼"**	68	136	204	272	340	408	476	544	612	680	748	816	884	952	1020	1088	1156	1224	1292	1360
2"	**2½"**	48	112	160	224	288	336	400	448	512	576	624	688	736	800	864	912	976	1024	1088	1152
2¼"	**2¾"**	42	84	126	182	224	266	308	364	406	448	504	546	588	630	686	728	770	812	868	910
2½"	**3"**	39	78	117	156	195	234	273	312	351	390	429	468	507	546	585	624	663	702	741	780
2¾"	**3¼"**	24	60	96	132	156	192	228	264	288	324	360	396	432	456	492	528	564	588	624	660
3"	**3½"**	22	55	77	110	132	165	198	220	253	275	308	330	363	396	418	451	473	506	528	561
3¼"	**3¾"**	20	40	70	90	120	140	160	190	210	240	260	280	310	330	360	380	400	430	450	480
3½"	**4"**	20	40	60	90	110	130	150	180	200	220	240	270	290	310	330	360	380	400	420	450
3¾"	**4¼"**	18	36	54	72	90	108	126	144	171	189	207	225	243	261	279	297	324	342	360	378
4"	**4½"**	16	32	48	64	80	96	112	128	144	160	176	192	208	224	240	256	272	288	304	320
4¼"	**4¾"**	8	24	40	56	72	88	104	120	136	144	160	176	192	208	224	240	256	272	288	296
4½"	**5"**	8	24	40	56	72	80	96	112	128	144	152	168	184	200	216	224	240	256	272	288
4¾"	**5¼"**	7	21	35	42	56	70	84	91	105	119	126	140	154	168	175	189	203	210	224	238
5"	**5½"**	7	21	28	42	56	63	77	91	98	112	126	133	147	154	168	182	189	203	217	224
5¼"	**5¾"**	6	18	24	36	42	54	60	72	84	90	102	108	120	126	138	150	156	168	174	186
5½"	**6"**	6	18	24	36	42	54	60	72	78	90	96	108	114	126	132	144	150	162	171	180
5¾"	**6¼"**	6	12	24	30	42	48	60	66	72	84	90	102	108	120	126	138	144	150	162	168
6"	**6½"**	6	12	24	30	36	48	54	66	72	78	90	96	108	114	120	132	138	144	156	162
6¼"	**6¾"**	5	10	20	25	30	40	45	50	60	65	70	80	85	90	100	105	110	120	125	130
6½"	**7"**	5	10	15	25	30	35	45	50	55	60	70	75	80	90	95	100	105	115	120	125
6¾"	**7¼"**	5	10	15	20	30	35	40	45	55	60	65	70	80	85	90	95	105	110	115	120
7"	**7½"**	5	10	15	20	30	35	40	45	50	60	65	70	75	80	90	95	100	105	110	120
7¼"	**7¾"**	5	10	15	20	25	30	40	45	50	55	60	65	75	80	85	90	95	100	110	115
7½"	**8"**	5	10	15	20	25	30	35	45	50	55	60	65	70	75	80	90	95	100	105	110
7¾"	**8¼"**	4	8	12	16	20	24	28	32	36	40	48	52	56	60	64	68	72	76	80	84
8"	**8½"**	4	8	12	16	20	24	28	32	36	40	44	48	52	56	60	64	72	76	80	84
8¼"	**8¾"**	4	8	12	16	20	24	28	32	36	40	44	48	52	56	60	64	68	72	76	80
8½"	**9"**	4	8	12	16	20	24	28	32	36	36	44	48	52	56	60	64	68	72	76	80
8¾"	**9¼"**		4	8	12	16	20	24	28	32	36	40	44	48	52	56	60	64	68	72	76
9"	**9½"**		4	8	12	16	20	24	28	32	36	40	44	48	52	56	60	64	68	72	72
9¼"	**9¾"**		4	8	12	16	20	24	28	32	36	40	44	48	48	52	56	60	64	68	72

Squares From Yardage

Finished Size	Cut Size	Approximate No. of Squares from Yardage																			
		¼ yd	½ yd	¾ yd	1 yd	1¼ yds	1½ yds	1¾ yds	2 yds	2¼ yds	2½ yds	2¾ yds	3 yds	3¼ yds	3½ yds	3¾ yds	4 yds	4¼ yds	4½ yds	4¾ yds	5 yds
9½"	**10"**		4	8	12	16	20	24	28	32	36	36	40	44	48	52	56	60	64	68	72
9¾"	**10¼"**		3	6	9	12	15	18	21	21	24	27	30	33	36	39	42	42	45	48	51
10"	**10½"**		3	6	9	12	15	18	18	21	24	27	30	33	36	36	39	42	45	48	51
10½"	**11"**		3	6	9	12	12	15	18	21	24	27	27	30	33	36	39	39	42	45	48
11"	**11½"**		3	6	9	9	12	15	18	21	21	24	27	30	30	33	36	39	42	42	45
11½"	**12"**		3	6	9	9	12	15	18	18	21	24	27	27	30	33	36	36	39	42	45
12"	**12½"**		3	6	6	9	12	15	15	18	21	21	24	27	30	30	33	36	36	39	42
12½"	**13"**		3	6	6	9	12	12	15	18	18	21	24	27	27	30	33	33	36	39	39
13"	**13½"**		2	4	4	6	8	8	10	12	12	14	16	16	18	20	20	22	24	24	26
13½"	**14"**		2	2	4	6	6	8	10	10	12	14	14	16	18	18	20	20	22	24	24
14"	**14½"**		2	2	4	6	6	8	8	10	12	12	14	16	16	18	18	20	22	22	24
14½"	**15"**		2	2	4	6	6	8	8	10	12	12	14	14	16	18	18	20	20	22	24
15"	**15½"**		2	2	4	4	6	8	8	10	10	12	12	14	16	16	18	18	20	22	22
15½"	**16"**		2	2	4	4	6	6	8	10	10	12	12	14	14	16	18	18	20	20	22
16	**16½"**		2	2	4	4	6	6	8	8	10	12	12	14	14	16	16	18	18	20	20
16½"	**17"**		2	2	4	4	6	6	8	8	10	10	12	12	14	14	16	18	18	20	20
17"	**17½"**		2	2	4	4	6	6	8	8	10	10	12	12	14	14	16	16	18	18	20
17½"	**18"**		2	2	4	4	6	6	8	8	10	10	12	12	14	14	16	16	18	18	20
18"	**18½"**			2	2	4	4	6	6	8	8	10	10	12	12	14	14	16	16	18	18

Squares From Precuts

Finished Size	Cut Size	Approximate No. of Squares From Precuts*						
		1½" x 42"	2½" x 42"	5" x 42"	5" x 5"	10" x 10"	16" x 16"	18" x 21"
1"	**1½"**	28	28	84	9	36	100	168
1¼"	**1¾"**		24	48	4	25	81	120
1½"	**2"**		21	42	4	25	64	90
1¾"	**2¼"**		18	36	4	16	49	72
2"	**2½"**		16	32	4	16	36	56
2¼"	**2¾"**			15	1	9	25	42
2½"	**3"**			14	1	9	25	42
2¾"	**3¼"**			12	1	9	16	30
3"	**3½"**			12	1	4	16	30
3¼"	**3¾"**			11	1	4	16	20
3½"	**4"**			10	1	4	16	20
3¾"	**4¼"**			9	1	4	9	16
4"	**4½"**			9	1	4	9	16
4¼"	**4¾"**			8	1	4	9	12
4½"	**5"**			8	1	4	9	12
4¾"	**5¼"**					1	9	12

*For more information about precuts, see page 2.

Squares From Precuts

Finished Size	Cut Size	Approximate No. of Squares From Precuts*						
		1½" x 42"	2½" x 42"	5" x 42"	5" x 5"	10" x 10"	16" x 16"	18" x 21"
5"	5½"					1	4	9
5¼"	5¾"					1	4	9
5½"	6"					1	4	9
5¾"	6¼"					1	4	6
6"	6½"					1	4	6
6¼"	6¾"					1	4	6
6½"	7"					1	4	6
6¾"	7¼"					1	4	4
7"	7½"					1	4	4
7¼"	7¾"					1	4	4
7½"	8"					1	4	4
7¾"	8¼"					1	1	4
8"	8½"					1	1	4
8¼"	8¾"					1	1	4
8½"	9"					1	1	4
8¾"	9¼"					1	1	2
9"	9½"					1	1	2
9¼"	9¾"					1	1	2
9½"	10"					1	1	2
9¾"	10¼"						1	2
10"	10½"						1	2
10½"	11"						1	1
11"	11½"						1	1
11½"	12"						1	1
12"	12½"						1	1
12½"	13"						1	1
13"	13½"						1	1
13½"	14"						1	1
14"	14½"						1	1
14½"	15"						1	1
15"	15½"						1	1
15½"	16"						1	1
16"	16½"							1
16½"	17"							1
17"	17½"							1
17½"	18"							1

*For more information about precuts, see page 2.

Half-Square Triangles

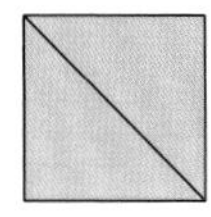
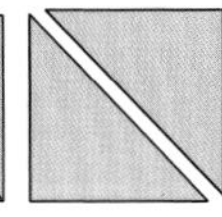
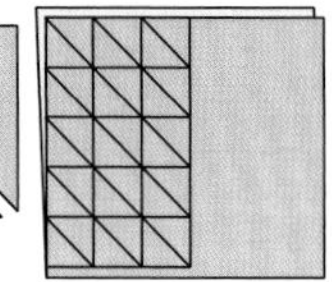

***Cutting Note:** This cutting layout shows the most efficient use of fabric. If using a rotary cutter (mat and ruler), cut strips the correct width; next cut squares, and then cut triangles. For templates, be sure to butt up the edges as in the drawing; trace and cut.*

Half-Square Triangles From Yardage

Finished Size	Cut Size	Approximate No. of Triangles From Yardage											
		¼ yd	½ yd	¾ yd	1 yd	1¼ yds	1½ yds	1¾ yds	2 yds	2¼ yds	2½ yds	2¾ yds	3 yds
1"	**1⅞"**	168	378	588	798	1008	1176	1386	1596	1806	2016	2184	2394
1¼"	**2⅛"**	144	288	432	576	756	900	1044	1188	1368	1512	1656	1800
1½"	**2⅜"**	96	224	352	480	576	704	832	960	1088	1184	1312	1440
1¾"	**2⅝"**	90	180	300	390	510	600	720	810	900	1020	1110	1230
2"	**2⅞"**	78	156	234	312	390	468	546	650	728	806	884	962
2¼"	**3⅛"**	48	120	192	264	336	408	480	552	600	672	744	816
2½"	**3⅜"**	44	110	176	220	286	352	396	462	528	572	638	704
2¾"	**3⅝"**	44	88	154	198	264	308	374	418	484	528	594	638
3"	**3⅞"**	40	80	120	180	220	260	320	360	400	460	500	540
3¼"	**4⅛"**	36	72	108	144	180	234	270	306	342	378	432	468
3½"	**4⅜"**	36	72	108	144	180	216	252	288	324	360	396	432
3¾"	**4⅝"**	16	48	80	112	144	176	208	240	272	304	336	368
4"	**4⅞"**	16	48	80	112	144	176	192	224	256	288	320	352
4¼"	**5⅛"**	14	42	70	98	112	140	168	196	210	238	266	294
4½"	**5⅜"**	14	42	70	84	112	140	154	182	210	224	252	280
4¾"	**5⅝"**	14	42	56	84	112	126	154	168	196	224	238	266
5"	**5⅞"**	12	36	48	72	84	108	120	144	156	180	192	216
5½"	**6⅜"**	12	24	48	60	84	96	108	132	144	168	180	192
6"	**6⅞"**	10	20	30	50	60	70	90	100	110	130	140	150
6½"	**7⅜"**	10	20	30	40	60	70	80	90	100	120	130	140
7"	**7⅞"**	10	20	30	40	50	60	80	90	100	110	120	130
7½"	**8⅜"**	8	16	24	32	40	48	56	64	72	80	88	96
8"	**8⅞"**	8	16	24	32	40	48	56	64	72	80	88	96
8½"	**9⅜"**		8	16	24	32	40	48	56	64	72	80	88
9"	**9⅞"**		8	16	24	32	40	48	56	64	72	80	80
9½"	**10⅜"**		6	12	18	24	30	36	36	42	48	54	60
10"	**10⅞"**		6	12	18	24	24	30	36	42	48	54	54
10½"	**11⅜"**		6	12	18	18	24	30	36	42	42	48	54
11"	**11⅞"**		6	12	18	18	24	30	36	36	42	48	54
11½"	**12⅜"**		6	12	12	18	24	30	30	36	42	48	48
12"	**12⅞"**		6	12	12	18	24	24	30	36	36	42	48
12½"	**13⅜"**		4	8	8	12	16	16	20	24	24	28	32
13"	**13⅞"**		4	4	8	12	12	16	20	20	24	28	28
13½"	**14⅜"**		4	4	8	12	12	16	20	20	24	24	28
14"	**14⅞"**		4	4	8	12	12	16	16	20	24	24	28
14½"	**15⅜"**		4	4	8	8	12	16	16	20	20	24	28

Half-Square Triangles From Precuts

Finished Size	Cut Size	Approximate No. of Triangles From Precuts*						
		1½" x 42"	2½" x 42"	5" x 42"	5" x 5"	10" x 10"	16" x 16"	18" x 21"
1"	1⅞"		22	44	4	25	64	99
1¼"	2⅛"		19	38	4	16	49	72
1½"	2⅜"		17	34	4	16	36	72
1¾"	2⅝"			16	1	9	36	48
2"	2⅞"			14	1	9	25	42
2¼"	3⅛"			13	1	9	25	30
2½"	3⅜"			12	1	4	16	30
2¾"	3⅝"			11	1	4	16	20
3"	3⅞"			10	1	4	16	20
3¼"	4⅛"			10	1	4	9	20
3½"	4⅜"			9	1	4	9	16
3¾"	4⅝"			9	1	4	9	12
4"	4⅞"			8	1	4	9	12
4¼"	5⅛"					1	9	12
4½"	5⅜"					1	4	9
4¾"	5⅝"					1	4	9
5"	5⅞"					1	4	9
5½"	6⅜"					1	4	6
6"	6⅞"					1	4	6
6½"	7⅜"					1	4	4
7"	7⅞"					1	4	4
7½"	8⅜"					1	1	4
8"	8⅞"					1	1	4
8½"	9⅜"					1	1	2
9"	9⅞"					1	1	2
9½"	10⅜"						1	2
10"	10⅞"						1	1
10½"	11⅜"						1	1
11"	11⅞"						1	1
11½"	12⅜"						1	1
12"	12⅞"						1	1
12½"	13⅜"						1	1
13"	13⅞"						1	1
13½"	14⅜"						1	1
14"	14⅞"						1	1
14½"	15⅜"						1	1

*For more information about precuts, see page 2.

Quarter-Square Triangles

Use this chart for triangles where the longest edge needs to be on the straight of grain, such as for setting triangles. For sizes not in the chart, add 1¼" to the finished size of the square (block) to determine the cut size. Use the next size up in the chart to estimate yardage.

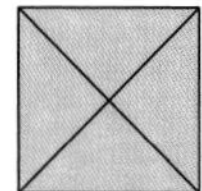

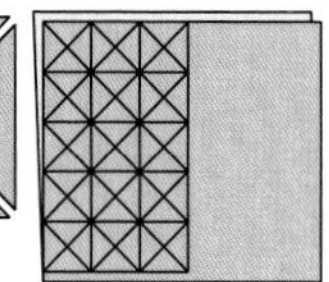

Cutting Note: *This cutting layout shows the most efficient use of fabric. If using a rotary cutter (mat and ruler), cut strips the correct width; next cut squares, and then cut triangles. For templates, be sure to butt up the edges as in the drawing; trace and cut.*

Quarter-Square Triangles From Yardage

Finished Size	Cut Size	Approximate No. of Triangles From Yardage							
		¼ yd	½ yd	¾ yd	1 yd	1¼ yds	1½ yds	1¾ yds	2 yds
1"	**2¼"**	272	544	816	1088	1360	1632	1904	2176
1¼"	**2½"**	192	448	640	896	1152	1344	1600	1792
1½"	**2¾"**	168	336	504	728	896	1064	1232	1456
1¾"	**3"**	156	312	468	624	780	936	1092	1248
2"	**3¼"**	96	240	384	528	624	768	912	1056
2¼"	**3½"**	88	220	308	440	528	660	792	880
2½"	**3¾"**	80	160	280	360	480	560	640	760
2¾"	**4"**	80	160	240	360	440	520	600	720
3"	**4¼"**	72	144	216	288	360	432	504	576
3¼"	**4½"**	64	128	192	256	320	384	448	512
3½"	**4¾"**	32	96	160	224	288	352	416	480
3¾"	**5"**	32	96	160	224	288	320	384	448
4"	**5¼"**	28	84	140	168	224	280	336	364
4¼"	**5½"**	28	84	112	168	224	252	308	364
4½"	**5¾"**	24	72	96	144	168	216	240	288
4¾"	**6"**	24	72	96	144	168	216	240	288
5"	**6¼"**	24	48	96	120	168	192	240	264
5¼"	**6½"**	24	48	96	120	144	192	216	264
5½"	**6¾"**	20	40	80	100	120	160	180	200
5¾"	**7"**	20	40	60	100	120	140	180	200
6"	**7¼"**	20	40	60	80	120	140	160	180
6¼"	**7½"**	20	40	60	80	120	140	160	180
6½"	**7¾"**	20	40	60	80	100	120	160	180
6¾"	**8"**	20	40	60	80	100	120	140	180
7"	**8¼"**	16	32	48	64	80	96	112	128
7¼"	**8½"**	16	32	48	64	80	96	112	128
7½"	**8¾"**	16	32	48	64	80	96	112	128
7¾"	**9"**	16	32	48	64	80	96	112	128
8"	**9¼"**		16	32	48	64	80	96	112
8¼"	**9½"**		16	32	48	64	80	96	112
8½"	**9¾"**		16	32	48	64	80	96	112
8¾"	**10"**		16	32	48	64	80	96	112
9"	**10¼"**		12	24	36	48	60	72	84
9½"	**10¾"**		12	24	36	48	60	60	72

Quarter-Square Triangles From Yardage

Finished Size	Cut Size	Approximate No. of Triangles From Yardage							
		¼ yd	½ yd	¾ yd	1 yd	1¼ yds	1½ yds	1¾ yds	2 yds
10"	**11¼"**		12	24	36	48	48	60	72
10½"	**11¾"**		12	24	36	48	48	60	72
11"	**12¼"**		12	24	24	48	48	60	60
11½"	**12¾"**		12	24	24	36	48	48	60
12"	**13¼"**		12	24	24	36	48	48	60
12½"	**13¾"**		8	8	16	24	24	32	40
13"	**14¼"**		8	8	16	24	24	32	40
13½"	**14¾"**		8	8	16	24	24	32	32
14"	**15¼"**		8	8	16	16	24	32	32
14½"	**15¾"**		8	8	16	16	24	32	32
15"	**16¼"**		8	8	16	16	24	24	32
15½"	**16¾"**		8	8	16	16	24	24	32
16"	**17¼"**		8	8	16	16	24	24	32
17"	**18¼"**			8	8	16	16	24	24
18"	**19¼"**			8	8	16	16	24	24
19"	**20¼"**			4	4	8	8	12	12
20"	**21¼"**			4	4	8	8	8	12

Quarter-Square Triangles From Precuts

Finished Size	Cut Size	Approximate No. of Triangles From Precuts*						
		1½" x 42"	2½" x 42"	5" x 42"	5" x 5"	10" x 10"	16" x 16"	18" x 21"
1"	**2¼"**		18	36	4	16	49	72
1¼"	**2½"**		16	32	4	16	36	56
1½"	**2¾"**			15	1	9	25	42
1¾"	**3"**			14	1	9	25	42
2"	**3¼"**			12	1	9	16	30
2¼"	**3½"**			12	1	4	16	30
2½"	**3¾"**			11	1	4	16	20
2¾"	**4"**			10	1	4	16	20
3"	**4¼"**			9	1	4	9	16
3¼"	**4½"**			9	1	4	9	16
3½"	**4¾"**			8	1	4	9	12
3¾"	**5"**			8	1	4	9	12
4"	**5¼"**					1	9	12
4¼"	**5½"**					1	4	9
4½"	**5¾"**					1	4	9
4¾"	**6"**					1	4	9
5"	**6¼"**					1	4	6
5¼"	**6½"**					1	4	6
5½"	**6¾"**					1	4	6
5¾"	**7"**					1	4	6

*For more information about precuts, see page 2.

Quarter-Square Triangles From Precuts

Finished Size	Cut Size	Approximate No. of Triangles From Precuts*						
		1½" x 42"	2½" x 42"	5" x 42"	5" x 5"	10" x 10"	16" x 16"	18" x 21"
6"	7¼"					1	4	4
6¼"	7½"					1	4	4
6½"	7¾"					1	4	4
6¾"	8"					1	4	4
7"	8¼"					1	1	4
7¼"	8½"					1	1	4
7½"	8¾"					1	1	4
7¾"	9"					1	1	4
8"	9¼"					1	1	2
8¼"	9½"					1	1	2
8½"	9¾"					1	1	2
8¾"	10"					1	1	2
9"	10¼"						1	2
9½"	10¾"						1	1
10"	11¼"						1	1
10½"	11¾"						1	1
11"	12¼"						1	1
11½"	12¾"						1	1
12"	13¼"						1	1
12½"	13¾"						1	1
13"	14¼"						1	1
13½"	14¾"						1	1
14"	15¼"						1	1
14½"	15¾"						1	1
15"	16¼"							1
15½"	16¾"							1
16"	17¼"							1
17"	18¼"							

*For more information about precuts, see page 2.

Sashing Strips

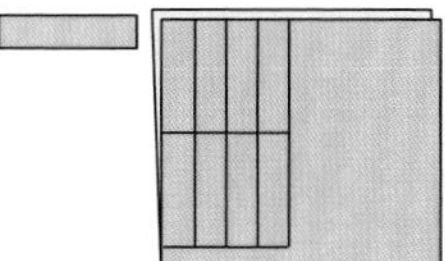

Cutting Note: *This cutting layout shows the most efficient use of fabric. If using a rotary cutter (mat and ruler), cut strips the correct width, and then cut to correct length. For templates, be sure to butt up the edges as in the drawing; trace and cut.*

Sashing Strips From Yardage

Finished Size	Cut Size	Approximate No. of Sashing Strips From Yardage											
		¼ yd	½ yd	¾ yd	1 yd	1¼ yds	1½ yds	1¾ yds	2 yds	2¼ yds	2½ yds	2¾ yds	3 yds
1" x 7"	**1½" x 7½"**	30	60	90	120	150	180	210	240	270	300	330	360
1" x 8"	**1½" x 8½"**	24	48	72	96	120	144	168	192	216	240	264	288
1" x 9"	**1½" x 9½"**	24	48	72	96	120	144	168	192	216	240	264	288
1" x 10"	**1½" x 10½"**	18	36	54	72	90	108	126	144	162	180	198	216
1" x 12"	**1½" x 12½"**	18	36	54	72	90	108	126	144	162	180	198	216
1" x 14"	**1½" x 14½"**	12	24	36	48	60	72	84	96	108	120	132	144
1" x 15"	**1½" x 15½"**	12	24	36	48	60	72	84	96	108	120	132	144
1" x 16"	**1½" x 16½"**	12	24	36	48	60	72	84	96	108	120	132	144
1" x 18"	**1½" x 18½"**	12	24	36	48	60	72	84	96	108	120	132	144
1½" x 7"	**2" x 7½"**	20	45	65	90	110	135	155	180	200	225	245	270
1½" x 8"	**2" x 8½"**	16	36	52	72	88	108	140	144	160	180	196	216
1½" x 9"	**2" x 9½"**	16	36	52	72	88	108	140	144	160	180	196	216
1½" x 10"	**2" x 10½"**	12	27	39	54	66	81	93	108	120	135	147	162
1½" x 12"	**2" x 12½"**	12	27	39	54	66	81	93	108	120	135	147	162
1½" x 14"	**2" x 14½"**	8	18	26	36	44	54	63	72	80	90	98	108
1½" x 15"	**2" x 15½"**	8	18	26	36	44	54	62	72	80	90	98	108
1½" x 16"	**2" x 16½"**	8	18	26	36	44	54	62	72	80	90	98	108
1½" x 18"	**2" x 18½"**	8	18	26	36	44	54	62	72	80	90	98	108
2" x 7"	**2½" x 7½"**	15	35	50	70	90	105	125	140	160	180	195	215
2" x 8"	**2½" x 8½"**	12	28	40	56	72	84	100	112	128	144	156	172
2" x 9"	**2½" x 9½"**	12	28	40	56	72	84	100	112	128	144	156	172
2" x 10"	**2½" x 10½"**	9	27	30	42	54	63	75	84	96	108	117	129
2" x 12"	**2½" x 12½"**	9	27	30	42	54	63	75	84	96	108	117	129
2" x 14"	**2½" x 14½"**	6	14	20	28	36	42	50	56	64	72	78	86
2" x 15"	**2½" x 15½"**	6	14	20	28	36	42	50	56	64	72	78	86
2" x 16"	**2½" x 16½"**	6	14	20	28	36	42	50	56	64	72	78	86
2" x 18"	**2½" x 18½"**	6	14	20	28	36	42	50	56	64	72	78	86
2½" x 7"	**3" x 7½"**	15	30	45	60	75	90	105	120	135	150	165	180
2½" x 8"	**3" x 8½"**	12	24	36	48	60	72	84	96	108	120	132	144
2½" x 9"	**3" x 9½"**	12	24	36	48	60	72	84	96	108	120	132	144
2½" x 10"	**3" x 10½"**	9	18	27	36	45	54	63	72	81	90	99	108
2½" x 12"	**3" x 12½"**	9	18	27	36	45	54	63	72	81	90	99	108
2½" x 14"	**3" x 14½"**	6	12	18	24	30	36	45	48	54	60	66	72
2½" x 15"	**3" x 15½"**	6	12	18	24	30	36	42	48	54	60	66	72
2½" x 16"	**3" x 16½"**	6	12	18	24	30	36	42	48	54	60	66	72
2½" x 18"	**3" x 18½"**	6	12	18	24	30	36	42	48	54	60	66	72

Sashing Strips From Yardage

Finished Size	Cut Size	Approximate No. of Sashing Strips From Yardage											
		¼ yd	½ yd	¾ yd	1 yd	1¼ yds	1½ yds	1¾ yds	2 yds	2¼ yds	2½ yds	2¾ yds	3 yds
3" x 7"	3½" x 7½"	10	25	35	50	60	75	90	100	115	125	140	150
3" x 8"	3½" x 8½"	8	20	28	40	48	60	72	80	92	100	112	120
3" x 9"	3½" x 9½"	8	20	28	40	48	60	72	80	92	100	112	120
3" x 10"	3½" x 10½"	6	15	21	30	36	45	54	60	69	75	84	90
3" x 12"	3½" x 12½"	6	15	21	30	36	45	54	60	69	75	84	90
3" x 14"	3½" x 14½"	4	10	14	20	24	30	36	40	46	50	56	60
3" x 15"	3½" x 15½"	4	10	14	20	24	30	36	40	46	50	56	60
3" x 16"	3½" x 16½"	4	10	14	20	24	30	36	40	46	50	56	60
3" x 18"	3½" x 18½"	4	10	14	20	24	30	36	40	46	50	56	60

For smaller sizes of strips, see Rectangles on page 24.

Sashing Strips From Precuts

Finished Size	Cut Size	Approximate No. of Sashing Strips From Precuts*						
		1½" x 42"	2½" x 42"	5" x 42"	5" x 5"	10" x 10"	16" x 16"	18" x 21"
1" x 7"	1½" x 7½"	5	5	15		6	20	24
1" x 8"	1½" x 8½"	4	4	12		6	10	24
1" x 9"	1½" x 9½"	4	4	12		6	10	24
1" x 10"	1½" x 10½"	4	4	12			10	24
1" x 12"	1½" x 12½"	3	3	9			10	12
1" x 14"	1½" x 14½"	2	2	6			10	12
1" x 15"	1½" x 15½"	2	2	6			10	12
1" x 16"	1½" x 16½"	2	2	6				12
1" x 18"	1½" x 18½"	2	2	6				12
1½" x 7"	2" x 7½"		5	10		5	16	18
1½" x 8"	2" x 8½"		4	8		5	8	18
1½" x 9"	2" x 9½"		4	8		5	8	18
1½" x 10"	2" x 10½"		4	8			8	18
1½" x 12"	2" x 12½"		3	6			8	9
1½" x 14"	2" x 14½"		2	4			8	9
1½" x 15"	2" x 15½"		2	4			8	9
1½" x 16"	2" x 16½"		2	4				9
1½" x 18"	2" x 18½"		2	4				9
2" x 7"	2½" x 7½"		5	10		4	12	14
2" x 8"	2½" x 8½"		4	8		4	6	14
2" x 9"	2½" x 9½"		4	8		4	6	14
2" x 10"	2½" x 10½"		4	8			6	14
2" x 12"	2½" x 12½"		3	6			6	7
2" x 14"	2½" x 14½"		2	4			6	7
2" x 15"	2½" x 15½"		2	4			6	7
2" x 16"	2½" x 16½"		2	4				7
2" x 18"	2½" x 18½"		2	4				7

*For more information about precuts, see page 2.

Sashing Strips From Precuts

Finished Size	Cut Size	Approximate No. of Sashing Strips From Precuts*						
		1½" x 42"	2½" x 42"	5" x 42"	5" x 5"	10" x 10"	16" x 16"	18" x 21"
2½" x 7"	3" x 7½"			5		3	10	12
2½" x 8"	3" x 8½"			4		3	5	12
2½" x 9"	3" x 9½"			4		3	5	12
2½" x 10"	3" x 10½"			4			5	12
2½" x 12"	3" x 12½"			3			5	6
2½" x 14"	3" x 14½"			2			5	6
2½" x 15"	3" x 15½"			2			5	6
2½" x 16"	3" x 16½"			2				6
2½" x 18"	3" x 18½"			2				6
3" x 7"	3½" x 7½"			5		2	8	10
3" x 8"	3½" x 8½"			4		2	4	10
3" x 9"	3½" x 9½"			4		2	4	10
3" x 10"	3½" x 10½"			4			4	10
3" x 12"	3½" x 12½"			3			4	5
3" x 14"	3½" x 14½"			2			4	5
3" x 15"	3½" x 15½"			2			4	5
3" x 16"	3½" x 16½"			2				5
3" x 18"	3½" x 18½"			2				5

*For more information about precuts, see page 2.
For smaller sizes of strips, see Rectangles on page 24.

Diamonds (60 degree)

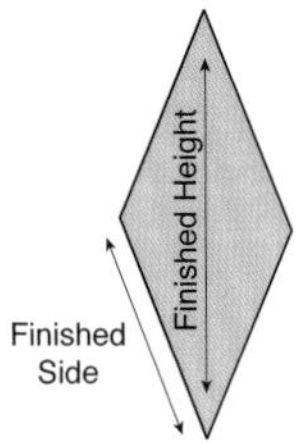

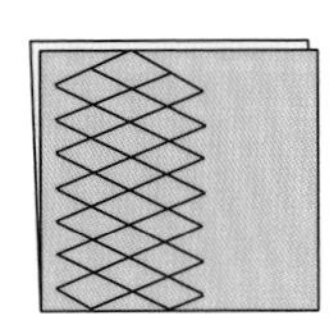

Cutting Note: *This cutting layout shows the most efficient use of fabric. If using a rotary cutter (mat and ruler), cut strips the correct width, and then cut diamonds. For templates, be sure to butt up the edges as in the drawing; trace and cut.*

60-Degree Diamonds From Yardage

Finished Side	Finished Height	Approximate No. of 60-Degree Diamonds From Yardage											
		¼ yd	½ yd	¾ yd	1 yd	1¼ yds	1½ yds	1¾ yds	2 yds	2¼ yds	2½ yds	2¾ yds	3 yds
1"	1¾"	120	288	432	600	744	912	1056	1224	1368	1536	1704	1848
1¼"	2³⁄₁₆"	82	205	308	431	533	656	759	902	984	1107	1210	1333
1½"	2⅝"	54	144	234	324	414	504	594	684	774	864	954	1044
1¾"	3"	48	112	192	256	320	400	464	528	608	672	752	816
2"	3½"	44	102	160	218	276	334	392	450	525	566	624	682
2¼"	3⅞"	26	78	117	169	221	260	312	351	403	455	494	546
2½"	4⁵⁄₁₆"	24	6	108	144	180	228	264	300	348	384	420	468
2¾"	4¾"	22	55	88	121	154	187	220	264	297	330	363	396
3"	5³⁄₁₆"	11	42	74	105	137	168	200	231	252	284	315	347
3½"	6¹⁄₁₆"	9	36	54	81	99	126	144	171	207	216	234	261
4"	7"	8	24	40	64	80	96	112	136	152	168	184	208
4½"	8"		14	28	42	56	70	84	98	112	126	140	154
5"	8⅝"		13	26	39	52	65	72	85	98	111	124	137
5½"	9⁹⁄₁₆"		12	24	30	42	54	66	72	84	96	102	114
6"	10⅜"		11	17	28	33	44	50	61	72	77	88	94

60-Degree Diamonds From Precuts

Finished Side	Finished Height	Approximate No. of 60-Degree Diamonds From Precuts*						
		1½" x 42"	2½" x 42"	5" x 42"	5" x 5"	10" x 10"	16" x 16"	18" x 21"
1"	1¾"			50	5	33	90	144
1¼"	2³⁄₁₆"			43	4	21	64	105
1½"	2⅝"			19	2	16	49	72
1¾"	3"			17	2	11	36	56
2"	3½"			16	1	9	33	53
2¼"	3⅞"			14	1	3	25	39
2½"	4⁵⁄₁₆"					3	18	30
2¾"	4¾"					2	16	28
3"	5³⁄₁₆"					2	14	20
3½"	6¹⁄₁₆"					2	9	18
4"	7"					2	8	12
4½"	8"					1	5	7
5"	8⅝"					1	2	3
5½"	9⁹⁄₁₆"						2	3
6"	10⅜"						2	3

*For more information about precuts, see page 2.

Diamonds (45 degree)

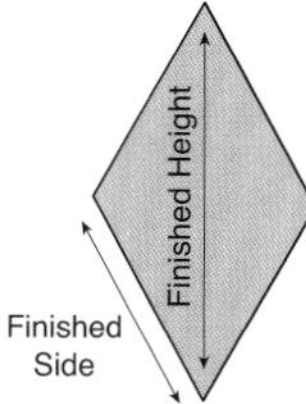

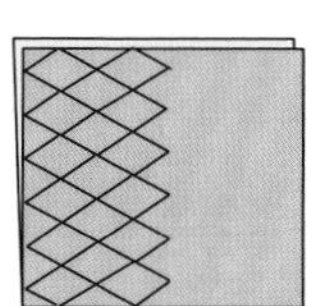

Cutting Note: *This cutting layout shows the most efficient use of fabric. If using a rotary cutter (mat and ruler), cut strips the correct width, and then cut diamonds. For templates, be sure to butt up the edges as in the drawing; trace and cut.*

45-Degree Diamonds From Yardage

Finished Side	Finished Height	Approximate No. of 45-Degree Diamonds From Yardage											
		¼ yd	½ yd	¾ yd	1 yd	1¼ yds	1½ yds	1¾ yds	2 yds	2¼ yds	2½ yds	2¾ yds	3 yds
1"	**1⅞"**	114	285	428	599	741	912	1055	1226	1368	1539	1682	1853
1¼"	**2 5/16"**	78	208	338	468	598	728	858	988	1118	1248	1378	1508
1½"	**2¾"**	66	154	264	352	440	550	660	726	836	924	1034	1122
1¾"	**3¼"**	41	123	205	287	369	451	533	615	697	759	841	923
2"	**3 11/16"**	36	114	162	234	306	360	432	486	576	630	684	756
2¼"	**4⅜"**	34	85	136	204	255	306	357	425	476	527	595	646
2½"	**4⅝"**	31	78	124	171	217	264	310	357	403	450	496	543
2¾"	**5⅛"**	14	56	98	140	168	210	252	294	322	364	406	448
3"	**5 9/16"**	13	52	78	117	156	182	221	260	286	325	351	390
3½"	**6½"**	12	46	58	92	115	138	173	196	219	242	276	299
4"	**7 7/16"**	11	32	53	74	95	116	137	158	179	200	221	242
4½"	**8 5/16"**		19	38	57	76	95	114	124	143	162	181	200
5"	**9 3/16"**		17	34	43	60	77	85	102	119	128	145	162
5½"	**10⅛"**		15	30	38	45	60	68	83	98	105	120	128
6"	**11 1/16"**		7	21	28	42	56	63	70	84	91	105	112

45-Degree Diamonds From Precuts

Finished Side	Finished Height	Approximate No. of 45-Degree Diamonds From Precuts*						
		1½" x 42"	2½" x 42"	5" x 42"	5" x 5"	10" x 10"	16" x 16"	18" x 21"
1"	**1⅞"**			60	6	33	88	145
1¼"	**2 5/16"**			28	3	24	70	108
1½"	**2¾"**			24	2	15	51	81
1¾"	**3¼"**			22	2	14	40	63
2"	**3 11/16"**			19	2	12	35	54
2¼"	**4⅜"**					7	26	43
2½"	**4⅝"**					4	22	38
2¾"	**5⅛"**					3	15	28
3"	**5 9/16"**					3	15	26
3½"	**6½"**					3	12	17
4"	**7 7/16"**					2	7	15
4½"	**8 5/16"**					2	7	9
5"	**9 3/16"**						3	8
5½"	**10⅛"**						3	4
6"	**11 1/16"**						3	4

*For more information about precuts, see page 2.

Borders

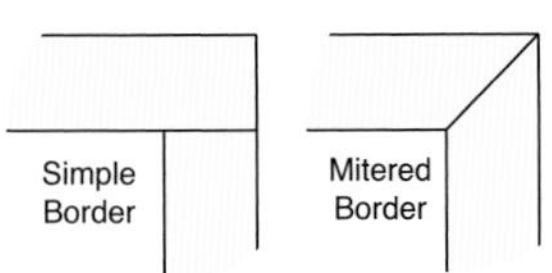

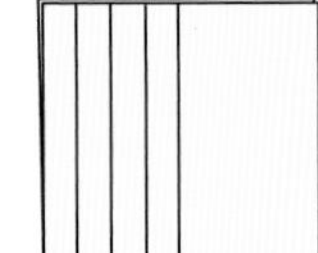

***Cutting Note:** Cut border strips as shown, and then piece if necessary to attain the necessary length.*

		Approximate Yardage												
	Finished Width	**½"**	**¾"**	**1"**	**1½"**	**2"**	**2½"**	**3"**	**3½"**	**4"**	**4½"**	**5"**	**5½"**	**6"**
	Cut Width	**1"**	**1¼"**	**1½"**	**2"**	**2½"**	**3"**	**3½"**	**4"**	**4½"**	**5"**	**5½"**	**6"**	**6½"**
Total Inches of Borders	**No. of Strips to Cut**													
160"	4	⅛	¼	¼	¼	⅜	⅜	½	½	½	⅝	⅝	⅝	¾
200"	5	¼	¼	¼	⅜	⅜	½	½	⅝	¾	¾	⅞	⅞	1
240"	6	¼	¼	¼	⅜	½	½	⅝	¾	¾	⅞	1	1	1⅛
280"	7	¼	¼	⅜	½	½	⅝	¾	⅞	⅞	1	1⅛	1¼	1⅜
320"	8	¼	⅜	⅜	½	⅝	¾	⅞	1	1	1⅛	1¼	1⅜	1½
360"	9	¼	⅜	⅜	½	⅝	¾	⅞	1	1⅛	1¼	1⅜	1½	1⅝
400"	10	⅜	⅜	½	⅝	¾	⅞	1	1⅛	1¼	1½	1⅝	1¾	1⅞
440"	11	⅜	½	½	¾	⅞	1	1⅛	1¼	1⅜	1⅝	1¾	1⅞	2
480"	12	⅜	½	½	¾	⅞	1	1¼	1⅜	1½	1¾	1⅞	2	2¼

Quilt Backing

***Example:** Your quilt measures 99" x 108". The closest measurement on the chart below is 100" x 110", therefore you would need 8¾ yards of fabric for the backing of your quilt.*

Quilt Size	Approximate Yardage
63" x 97"	5¾ yds
67" x 99"	5⅞ yds
71" x 101"	6 yds
75" x 103"	6 yds
79" x 105"	7 yds
78" x 97"	7 yds
82" x 99"	7¼ yds
86" x 101"	7½ yds
90" x 103"	7⅞ yds
94" x 105"	8¼ yds
84" x 102"	7½ yds
88" x 104"	7¾ yds
92" x 106"	8 yds
96" x 108"	8⅜ yds
100" x 110"	8¾ yds
100" x 102"	8¾ yds
104" x 104"	9 yds
109" x 106"	9¼ yds

Quilt Size	Approximate Yardage
112" x 108"	9⅜ yds
116" x 110"	10 yds

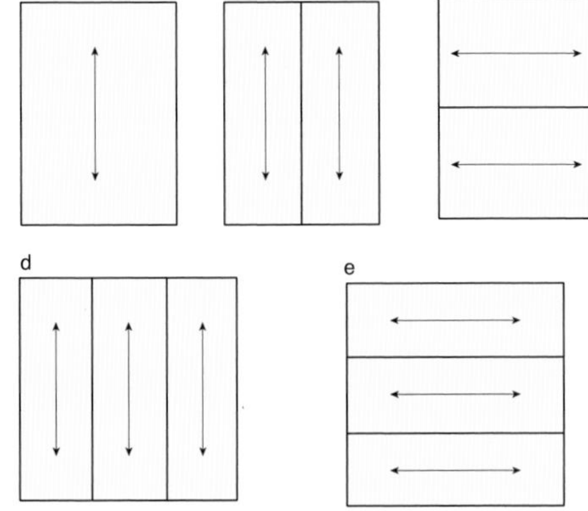

***Cutting Note:** These layouts show the most efficient use of fabric. In **b**, **c**, **d** and **e**, equal lengths are cut and sewn together to achieve the necessary size. The arrows indicate lengthwise grain.*

Diagonal Measurement of Blocks

Block Size	Diagonal Measurement
1"	1⅜"
1½"	2⅛"
2"	2¾"
2½"	3½"
3"	4¼"
3½"	5"
4"	5⅝"
4½"	6⅜"
5"	7¹⁄₁₆"
5½"	7¾"
6"	8½"
6½"	9³⁄₁₆"
7"	9⅞"
7½"	10⅝"
8"	11⁵⁄₁₆"

Block Size	Diagonal Measurement
8½"	12"
9"	12¾"
9½"	13⁷⁄₁₆"
10"	14⅛"
10½"	14⅞"
11"	15½"
11½"	16¼"
12"	17"
12½"	17¹¹⁄₁₆"
13"	18⅜"
13½"	19¹⁄₁₆"
14"	19¾"
14½"	20½"
15"	21⅛"
15½"	21¹⁵⁄₁₆"
16"	22⅝"
16½"	23⁵⁄₁₆"
17"	24"
17½"	24¾"
18"	25⁷⁄₁₆"
18½"	26³⁄₁₆"
19"	26⅞"
19½"	27⁹⁄₁₆"
20"	28¼"
20½"	29"
21"	29¹¹⁄₁₆"
21½"	30⅜"

Batting

Batting comes in many types and sizes. You can buy batting off the bolt or packaged. If buying off the bolt, the width varies from 22"–120". To achieve the size comparable to the packaged batting, use the following yardage chart.

Packaged Batting Labels	Crib	Twin	Full	Queen	King
Packaged Batting Sizes	**45" x 60"**	**72" x 90"**	**81" x 96"**	**90" x 108"**	**120" x 120"**
45"	1¾ yds	4 yds	5½ yds	6 yds	10 yds
48"	1¾ yds	4 yds	4½ yds	6 yds	10 yds
54"	1¾ yds	4 yds	4½ yds	5 yds	10 yds
90"	1¼ yds	2 yds	2¼ yds	3 yds	6¾ yds

Binding

Cutting Note: *Cut binding strips as shown, and then piece if necessary to attain the necessary length.*

Double-Fold Binding (Straight Grain)

		Yardage for Double-Fold Binding		
	Cut Width	**2"**	**2¼"**	**2½"**
Total Inches of Binding	**No. Strips to Cut**			
160"	4	¼ yd	¼ yd	⅜ yd
200"	5	⅓ yd	⅜ yd	⅜ yd
240"	6	⅜ yd	⅜ yd	½ yd
280"	7	½ yd	½ yd	½ yd
320"	8	½ yd	½ yd	⅝ yd
360"	9	½ yd	⅝ yd	⅝ yd
400"	10	⅝ yd	⅝ yd	¾ yd
440"	11	⅝ yd	¾ yd	⅞ yd
480"	12	⅔ yd	¾ yd	⅞ yd

Single-Fold Binding (Straight Grain)

		Yardage for Single-Fold Binding	
	Cut Width	**1¼"**	**1½"**
Total Inches of Binding	**No. Strips to Cut**		
160"	4	¼ yd	¼ yd
200"	5	¼ yd	¼ yd
240"	6	¼ yd	¼ yd
280"	7	¼ yd	⅜ yd
320"	8	⅜ yd	⅜ yd
360"	9	⅜ yd	⅜ yd
400"	10	⅜ yd	½ yd
440"	11	½ yd	½ yd
480"	12	½ yd	½ yd

Bias Binding

	Yardage for Bias Binding				
Cut Width of Binding	**1¼"**	**1½"**	**2"**	**2¼"**	**2½"**
Size of Square					
16"	192"	160"	128"	112"	102"
18"	252"	216"	162"	144"	129"
20"	320"	260"	200"	160"	160"
22"	374"	308"	242"	198"	193"
24"	456"	384"	288"	240"	230"
26"		442"	338"	286"	270"
28"			392"	336"	313"
30"			450"	390"	360"
32"			512"	448"	409"
34"			578"	510"	462"
36"				576"	518"
38"					577"
40"					640"
42"					705"

Making Continuous Bias Binding

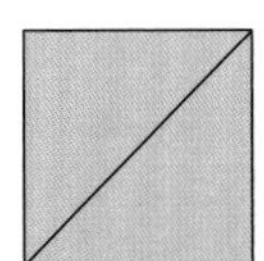

Cut square in half on one diagonal.

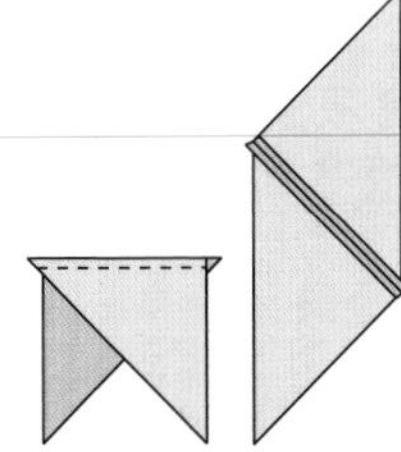

Sew the two halves with right sides together as shown using a ¼" seam allowance. Press seam open.

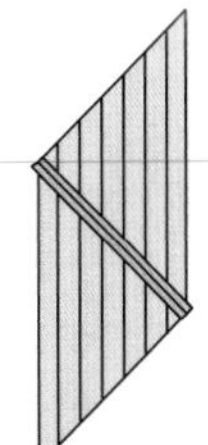

Draw lines spaced the cut width of binding on wrong side of fabric. Trim excess fabric, if necessary. Press seam open.

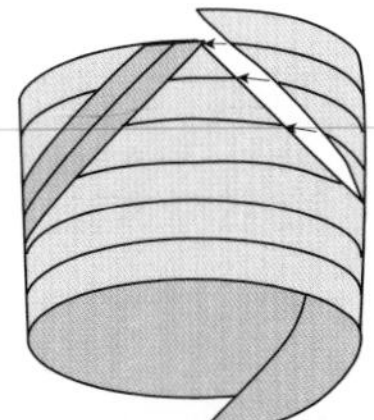

With drawn lines on the outside, bring diagonal edges toward each other to form a tube. Match lines, offsetting by one width. Join the diagonal edges with a ¼" seam allowance; press seam open.

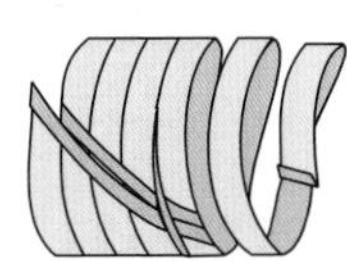

Cut along drawn lines to form a continuous bias binding strip.

Metric Conversions

Yards	Yards in Decimal	Inches	Meters	Centimeters
1⁄16	.0625	2¼"	0.057	5.72
⅛	0.125	4½"	0.114	11.43
3⁄16	0.1875	6¾"	0.171	17.15
¼	0.25	9"	0.229	22.86
5⁄16	0.3125	11¼"	0.286	28.58
⅜	0.375	13½"	0.343	34.29
7⁄16	0.4375	15¾"	0.4	40.01
½	0.5	18"	0.457	45.72
9⁄16	0.5625	20¼"	0.514	51.44
⅝	0.625	22½"	0.572	57.15
11⁄16	0.6875	24¾"	0.629	62.87
¾	0.75	27"	0.686	68.58
13⁄16	0.8125	29¼"	0.743	74.3
⅞	0.875	31½"	0.8	80.01
15⁄16	0.9375	33¾"	0.857	85.73
1	1.0	36"	0.914	91.44
1⅛	1.125	40½"	1.029	102.87
1¼	1.25	45"	1.143	114.3
1⅜	1.375	49½"	1.257	125.73
1½	1.5	54"	1.372	137.16
1⅝	1.625	58½"	1.486	148.59
1¾	1.75	63"	1.6	160.02
1⅞	1.875	67½"	1.715	171.45
2	2.0	72"	1.829	182.88

Yards	Yards in Decimal	Inches	Meters	Centimeters
2⅛	2.125	76½"	1.943	194.31
2¼	2.25	81"	2.057	205.74
2⅜	2.375	85½"	2.172	217.17
2½	2.5	90"	2.286	228.6
2⅝	2.625	94½"	2.4	240.03
2¾	2.75	99"	2.515	251.46
2⅞	2.875	103½"	2.629	262.89
3	3.0	108"	2.743	274.32
3⅛	3.125	112½"	2.858	285.75
3¼	3.25	117"	2.972	297.18
3⅜	3.375	121½"	3.086	308.61
3½	3.5	126"	3.2	320.04
3⅝	3.625	130½"	3.315	331.47
3¾	3.75	135"	3.429	342.9
3⅞	3.875	139½"	3.543	354.33
4	4.0	144"	3.658	365.76
4⅛	4.125	148½"	3.772	377.19
4¼	4.25	153"	3.886	388.62
4⅜	4.375	157½"	4	400.05
4½	4.5	162	4.115	411.48
4⅝	4.625	166½"	4.229	422.91
4¾	4.75	171"	4.34	434.34
4⅞	4.875	175½"	4.458	445.77
5	5	180"	4.572	457.2

E-mail: Customer_Service@whitebirches.com

Revised Patchwork Minus Mathwork is published by DRG, 306 East Parr Road, Berne, IN 46711, telephone (260) 589-4000. Printed in USA.

RETAIL STORES: If you would like to carry this pattern book or any other DRG publications, call the Wholesale Department at Annie's Attic to set up a direct account: (903) 636-4303. Also, request a complete listing of publications available from DRG.

ISBN: 978-1-59217-280-1
2 3 4 5 6 7 8 9

Quilt Worksheet

Once you have chosen the quilt block(s) for your quilt, use this worksheet to figure yardage amounts. Then, write in the amounts on the **Shopping List** found on page 48. Refer to **How Much Fabric to Buy** beginning on page 5 to follow the instructions for our example quilt.

Standard Mattress Size ______________________ (Refer to chart on page 9 or use your own measurement.)

Quilt Size (including drop) ______________________ (Refer to chart on page 9 for suggested sizes. For more sizes, see **Quilt Sizes & Number of Blocks** (charts starting on page 10).

Block Fabric

Block Finished Size ________________ **No. of Blocks in Quilt** ________________

Divide block into units (squares, triangles, rectangles, diamonds) and multiply by the number of blocks per quilt; then decide fabric colors and whether it will be light, medium, dark or in between. Then find yardage amounts in **Figuring Yardage** charts on pages 24–43.

No. of squares per block ______ per quilt _____ cut size _____ fabric _____ _____ yards
No. of squares per block ______ per quilt _____ cut size _____ fabric _____ _____ yards
No. of squares per block ______ per quilt _____ cut size _____ fabric _____ _____ yards
No. of squares per block ______ per quilt _____ cut size _____ fabric _____ _____ yards
No. of squares per block ______ per quilt _____ cut size _____ fabric _____ _____ yards

No. of triangles per block ______ per quilt _____ cut size _____ fabric _____ _____ yards
No. of triangles per block ______ per quilt _____ cut size _____ fabric _____ _____ yards
No. of triangles per block ______ per quilt _____ cut size _____ fabric _____ _____ yards
No. of triangles per block ______ per quilt _____ cut size _____ fabric _____ _____ yards
No. of triangles per block ______ per quilt _____ cut size _____ fabric _____ _____ yards

No. of rectangles per block _____ per quilt _____ cut size _____ fabric _____ _____ yards
No. of rectangles per block _____ per quilt _____ cut size _____ fabric _____ _____ yards
No. of rectangles per block _____ per quilt _____ cut size _____ fabric _____ _____ yards

Border Fabric

Simple Borders

First Border

Quilt center size (width by length) ______________________ (example: 70" x 90")

Border width: Finished size _____________ Cut size _____________

Sides (quilt length + quilt length): _____________ + _____________ = _____________

Top and bottom (quilt width + quilt width + 4 x finished width of side border):

________ + ________ + 4 x finished side border width ________ = ________

Total length of border strips needed (sides + top and bottom): ________ + ________ = ________ total inches for first border (refer to yardage chart for **Borders**, page 40, to convert inches to yardage amount)

Second Border

Quilt size including first border (width by length) ______________________

Border width: Finished size _____________ Cut size _____________

Sides (quilt length + quilt length): _____________ + _____________ = _____________

Top and bottom (quilt width + quilt width + 4 x finished width of side border):

________ + ________ + 4 x finished side border width ________ = ________

Total length of border strips needed (sides + top and bottom): ________ + ________ = ________ total inches for second border (refer to yardage chart for **Borders**, page 40, to convert inches to yardage amount)

Third Border

Quilt size including first and second borders (width by length) ______________________

Border width: Finished size _____________ Cut size _____________

Sides (quilt length + quilt length): _____________ + _____________ = _____________

Top and bottom (quilt width + quilt width + 4 x finished width of side border):

________ + ________ + 4 x finished side border width ________ = ________

Total length of border strips needed (sides + top and bottom): ________ + ________ = ________ total inches for third border (refer to yardage chart for **Borders**, page 40, to convert inches to yardage amount)

Mitered Borders

First Border

Quilt center size (width by length) ______________________ (example: 70" x 90")

Border width: Finished size _____________ Cut size _____________

Sides (length + 2 x finished border width + 4" x 2):

_____________ + _____________ + 4" = _____________ x 2 = _____________ total inches for both side borders

Top and bottom (length + 2 x finished width of border + 4" x 2):

_____________ + _____________ + 4" = _____________ x 2 = _____________ total inches for top and bottom borders

Total length of border strips needed (sides + top and bottom): ________ + ________ = ________ total inches for first border (refer to yardage chart for **Borders**, page 40, to convert inches to yardage amount)

Second Border

Quilt center size including first border (width by length) _______________________

Border width: Finished size _______________ Cut size _______________

Sides (length + 2 x finished top border width + 4" x 2):

_______________ + _______________ + 4" = _______________ x 2 = _______________ total inches for both side borders

Top and bottom (length + 2 x finished width of border + 4" x 2):

_______________ + _______________ + 4" = _______________ x 2 = _______________ total inches for top and bottom borders

Total length of border strips needed (sides + top and bottom): _________ + _________ = _________ total inches for second border (refer to yardage chart for **Borders**, page 40, to convert inches to yardage amounts)

Third Border

Quilt center size including first and second borders (width by length) _______________________

Border width: Finished size _______________ Cut size _______________

Sides (length + 2 x finished top border width + 4" x 2):

_______________ + _______________ + 4" = _______________ x 2 = _______________ total inches for both side borders

Top and bottom (length + 2 x finished width of border + 4 x 2):

_______________ + _______________ + 4" = _______________ x 2 = _______________ total inches for top and bottom borders

Total length of border strips needed (sides + top and bottom): _________ + _________ = _________ total inches for third border (refer to yardage chart for **Borders**, page 40, to convert inches to yardage amounts)

Backing Fabric

See yardage chart for **Quilt Backing**, page 40 _______________________

Batting

See yardage chart for **Batting**, page 41 _______________________

Double-Fold or Single-Fold Binding

Quilt size (width by length): _______________ (example: 70" x 90")

Binding cut width _______________________

Side + side + top + bottom + 12" (for insurance):

_________ + _________ + _________ + _________ + 12" = _________ total inches for binding (refer to yardage chart for **Binding** chart on page 42, to convert inches to yardage amounts)

Bias Binding

Quilt interior measurement (width by length): _______________ (example: 70" x 90")

Binding cut width _______________________

Side + side + top + bottom + 12" (for insurance)

_________ + _________ + _________ + _________ + 12" = _________ = total inches for binding. Go to **Bias Binding** chart on page 43, and find the closest total inches to the amount needed (use higher number). Go to top row to find finished width of binding, then look along the far left row to find the size square needed to cut to make total inches of binding strips.

Shopping List

Use yardage charts, pages 24–43 and your Quilt Worksheet calculations to fill amounts for your shopping list. Then place a swatch of fabric next to the fabric number to keep track of your fabric choices.

Remember to add ¼ yard to all listed yardage when purchasing the fabric.

Fabric Yardage	Fabric Swatch	Fabric Yardage	Fabric Swatch
Fabric 1 ____________yards		Fabric 8 ____________yards	
Fabric 2 ____________yards		First Border _________yards	
Fabric 3 ____________yards		Second Border _______yards	
Fabric 4 ____________yards		Third Border _________yards	
Fabric 5 ____________yards		Backing Fabric_______yards	
Fabric 6 ____________yards		Binding Fabric_______yards	
Fabric 7 ____________yards		Batting _____________yards	